A Short History of Denver

A SHORT HISTORY OF

Denver

STEPHEN J. LEONARD AND THOMAS J. NOEL

UNIVERSITY OF NEVADA PRESS   RENO & LAS VEGAS

University of Nevada Press, Reno, Nevada 89557 USA
Copyright © 2016 by University of Nevada Press
www.unpress.nevada.edu
All rights reserved
Manufactured in the United States of America
Cover photograph: iStock.com/gcosoveanu
Frontispiece: Denver skyline with mountain backdrop. Courtesy Tom Noel Collection

LIBRARY OF CONGRESS CATALOGING-IN-PUBLICATION DATA
Names: Leonard, Stephen J., 1941– author. | Noel, Thomas J. (Thomas Jacob), author.
Title: A short history of Denver / Stephen J. Leonard and Thomas J. Noel.
Description: Reno : University of Nevada Press, 2016. | Includes bibliographical references
and index.
Identifiers: LCCN 2016005517 (print) | LCCN 2016006506 (ebook) |
ISBN 978-1-943859-19-1 (pbk. : alk. paper) | ISBN 978-0-87417-003-0 (e-book)
Subjects: LCSH: Denver (Colo.)—History. | Denver Metropolitan Area (Colo.)—History.
Classification: LCC F784.D457 47 2016 (print) | LCC F784.D457 (ebook) | DDC
978.8/83—dc23
LC record available at http://lccn.loc.gov/2016005517

The paper used in this book meets the requirements of American National Standard for
Information Sciences—Permanence of Paper for Printed Library Materials, ANSI/NISO
Z39.48-1992 (R2002). Binding materials were selected for strength and durability.

FIRST PRINTING

For my sister-in-law, Gloria,
and my brother, Mark, for keeping
me patched together and for Vi Noel
for doing the same for Tom.

—Stephen J. Leonard

For Vi Noel and for all my
wonderful students, who, I suspect,
have taught me more than
I have taught them.

—Thomas J. Noel

Contents

Preface

$\mathcal{F}$or more than ten thousand years, people have lived at the base of the Rocky Mountains where Cherry Creek enters the South Platte River. Beginning in 1858, a town named Denver grew up there, mushrooming from fewer than 5,000 people in 1860 to what the US Census Bureau today calls the Denver-Aurora-Lakewood Metropolitan Statistical Area, with a population of more than 2.7 million. Add to that the more than 300,000 people in the adjoining Boulder Metropolitan Statistical Area, and the regional population exceeds 3 million, spread over thousands of square miles. Denver itself, with 600,158 people, ranked as the nation's twenty-sixth-largest city in 2010, and Aurora, to Denver's east, emerged as a sister city, boasting a population of more than 325,000, putting it fifty-sixth nationally.

Shoehorning all those people and that long sweep of time into the space allocated to this *Short History* has been challenging. Jerome Smiley, who wrote a Denver history in 1901, took 978 pages to do the job, and he has been faulted for not giving enough space to women and minorities. In 1990, when we wrote *Denver Mining Camp to Metropolis,* we struggled to fit the city's past into 544 oversize pages. The indefatigable Phil Goodstein has alone produced probably more than 5,000 pages on the city, and Tom Noel has devoted many of his forty-nine (counting this one) authored or coauthored books to Denver. Scores of other writers have sliced, diced, and summarized the story of Denver and its suburbs.

Obviously and regrettably, we have been forced to leave out much. In deciding what to include, we created imaginary readers and wrote the book for them. Some of our target readers may have grown up in Denver but never formally studied Denver or Colorado history. Or they may have learned it, forgotten it, and now need a refresher. Many of our imagined readers are among the hundreds of thousands of people who have been born in the Denver area in the past half century or have moved here from elsewhere. They may have picked up scraps of local lore. They perhaps know a little about the Arapaho and Cheyenne Indians who occupied the region before being driven away by gold seekers. They may have heard of John Evans because he has a prominent mountain west of the city named for him. They may have learned of the scandal and pathos surrounding the lives of Horace and Baby Doe Tabor. A goodly number of them know of Buffalo Bill (William Cody), the frontier scout turned showman whose spirit peers out over the city from his grave atop Lookout Mountain. Virtually all of them are aware of the Denver Broncos.

Partly, this book attempts to give greater substance and context to what many readers already know. Partly it aims to inform them of what they do not know by introducing them to some of the movers and shakers, heroes and villains, who shaped the city. It offers an overview of major events in the city's past, and it recognizes that Denver's history, especially its recent history, is the story of a metropolitan area with many communities rather than that of a single city.

We might have crammed *Short History* full of names and dates and risked putting imaginary readers to sleep. Instead, we have tried to reduce a Pikes Peak of information to a climbable hill. We go into detail about some aspects of the city's past and omit or downplay others. We mention hundreds of noteworthy people but exclude thousands. For the annals of public utilities, stirring tales about wastewater disposal schemes, and colorful accounts of taxation policies, readers must look elsewhere. We hope they will find this book a palatable, not overly filling appetizer, triggering their hunger for more Denver history. In the chapter on historic preservation, we suggest where to look for the past. In the list of sources, we mention books that have helped us make this book and will give those readers who want to learn more a place to dig deeper.

Finally, in constructing imaginary readers, we have kept in mind teachers and Denver history buffs. The teachers may need a place to go to find a brief account of local history so they speak intelligently to their classes. The buffs will know much of what they read here but may need to fill in a few gaps. We leave it to you, esteemed readers, to judge how successful we have been in making a long story short.

Acknowledgments

*M*any people made this book possible. At the Denver Public Library's Western History and Genealogy Department, hats off to manager Jim Kroll and crackerjack librarians Wendell Cox, Kellen Cutsworth, Erin Edwards, Craig Haggit, Bruce Hanson, Joan Harms, Abby Hoverstock, James Jeffery, and Jamie Seemiller. Photo librarian Coi Drummond Gehrig worked her usual magic. At the Stephen Hart Library at History Colorado, thanks to librarians Pat Fraker, Sarah Gilmor, and Melissa VanOtterloo; library director Laura Ruttum Senturia; library services technician Kasey Brooks; and staff photographer Jay DiLorenzo. Auraria Library archivist Rosemary Evetts assisted us, and we also appreciate librarian Ellen Metter's and library director Mary Somerville's support of local history. Many thanks to the libraries, museums, and photographers credited in the image captions for the images they have provided. Photographers Glenn Aultman, Glenn Cuerden, Sandra Dallas, Michael Gamer, Virginia Simmons, and Roger Whitacre have kindly allowed use of their art.

At Metropolitan State, History Department students, faculty, and staff have shared knowledge and offered help. Thanks to faculty members Owen Chariton, Vincent C. de Baca, James Drake, Peg Ekstrand, Derek Everett, Debra Faulkner, Meg Frisbee, Dolph Grundman, Frank Harper, R. Todd Laugen, Matt Makley, Laura McCall, John Monnett, Frank W. Nation, Kevin Rucker, and Ellen Slatkin. By fostering scholarly endeavor, Metropolitan State president Stephen Jordan, provost Vicki Golich, deputy provost Luis Torres, dean Joan L. Foster, associate dean Art Campa, and administrative staff members Gloria Kennison, Donna Potempa, Sharon Roehling, Chrystyna Banks, and Vince Werner helped make this book possible.

Students and former students at the University of Colorado (cu) at Denver, including Kathleen Barlow, Dana EchoHawk, Marcia Goldstein, Craig Leavitt, Kara Miyagishima, Judy Morley, Mary Rozinski O'Neil, Katy Ordway, Kirby Page-Schmit, Nicholas Wharton, and Amy Zimmer, helped refine this work. University of Colorado–Denver faculty members Chris Agee, Thomas Andrews, Ryan Crewe, Jay Fell, Mark Foster, Rebecca Hunt, Pam Laird, Myra Rich, Jim Walsh, and Jim Whiteside also enhanced our knowledge of Colorado. The debt we owe to others is partially acknowledged in the bibliography section. Among those many scholars, Phil Goodstein, one of the most knowledgeable, has given us tips and pointed out errors. Bill Philpott of the University of Denver (du), another walking encyclopedia, gave us a superb critique of our original manuscript that led to numerous improvements. Finally, we thank copy editor Annette Wenda; Matt Becker, former senior acquisitions editor at the University of Nevada Press; press director Justin Race, who patiently guided us, and production manager Jinni Fontana.

Timeline

References are to events in Denver unless another locale is specified.

12,000 BCE   Nomadic groups begin hunting along the Front Range.

ca. 1800   Cheyenne and Arapaho enter Colorado. Southern Arapaho begin winter camping on the site of Denver.

1803   The United States acquires French claims to northeastern Colorado, including the future site of Denver, as part of the Louisiana Purchase. Areas south of the Arkansas River and west of the Continental Divide are claimed by Spain until 1821, when Mexico assumes Spain's claims.

1820   Major Stephen H. Long explores eastern Colorado, including the future site of Denver. He labels it the "Great American Desert," unfit for white settlement.

1830s   Louis Vasquez establishes a fur trading post at the confluence of the South Platte River and Clear Creek.

1848   By the terms of the Treaty of Guadalupe Hidalgo, the United States takes over Mexican claims to the parts of Colorado not purchased from France in 1803.

1850   On June 22 a group of Cherokee Indians on their way to California make a small gold discovery in Ralston Creek, in present-day Arvada.

1851   The United States signs the Treaty of Fort Laramie with the Cheyenne, Arapaho, and other tribes of the northern plains. It confirms Cheyenne and Arapaho ownership of a huge tract of land, including the future site of Denver.

1857   At the Mexican Diggings near West Florida Avenue and the South Platte River, Hispanics find gold. A group of Missourians also reports gold discoveries that year.

1858	William Green Russell party from Auraria, Georgia, discovers gold in the South Platte River and establishes the town of Auraria in October. This and other discoveries in 1858 trigger the 1859 gold rush.
	Denver City founded by the William H. Larimer Jr. party on November 22.
1859	Boulder City Town Company established on February 10.
	On April 23, William N. Byers publishes the first issue of the *Rocky Mountain News,* Colorado's first newspaper.
	Golden founded on June 16.
1860	Auraria and Denver celebrate their merger on the Larimer Street Bridge over Cherry Creek on April 6.
1861	Colorado Territory created.
1863	Fire destroys much of Denver's business district.
1864	Cherry Creek flood devastates Denver.
	The Third Regiment of the Colorado Volunteers massacres an estimated 163 Cheyenne and Arapaho at Sand Creek on November 29.
1867	The territorial legislature selects Denver as the capital of the Colorado Territory, replacing Golden.
1870	The Denver Pacific, Kansas Pacific, and Colorado Central Railroads reach Denver, ending the town's isolation and stagnation.
	William Jackson Palmer organizes the Denver and Rio Grande Railroad, which eventually links Denver to far-flung places in Colorado, including Colorado Springs, Pueblo, Leadville, Alamosa, Durango, Ouray, and Grand Junction.
1871	The first streetcar line opens between Auraria and Five Points.
1873	Adolph Coors establishes Coors Brewing Company in Golden.
1874	The Colorado School of Mines opens in Golden.
1876	Colorado becomes the thirty-eighth state on August 1.
1877	The University of Colorado opens in Boulder.
1880s	Colorado's first great boom, propelled by mining and railroads, shoots Denver's population to 106,713 in 1890.
1891	Donald Fletcher founds the town of Fletcher, east of Denver. In 1907 it becomes Aurora.
1893	The silver crash sends the city and state into depression.

	Women gain the right to vote in all elections in Colorado, making Denver the largest city in the United States allowing equal suffrage.
1894	Boulder suffers a serious flood.
1902	City and County of Denver carved out of Arapahoe County.
1904–18	Mayor Robert W. Speer transforms Denver into a City Beautiful.
1908	The Democratic National Convention meets in early July at the new City Auditorium to nominate William Jennings Bryan for president.
1913	A storm dumps nearly four feet of snow on the city on December 1–5.
1913–16	Denver experiments with a commission form of government.
1916	Colorado begins statewide prohibition of alcohol.
1918–19	An influenza epidemic kills more than fourteen hundred in Denver.
1920	Strikebreakers kill seven bystanders during the Denver Tramway strike.
1923	Benjamin F. Stapleton, a member of the Ku Klux Klan, elected mayor.
1925	Mayor Stapleton helps destroy the local Klan.
1929	Denver Municipal (later renamed Stapleton) Airport opens.
1936	Western-slope water begins flowing to Denver through the Pioneer Bore of the Moffat Tunnel.
1941	The city opens Red Rocks outdoor amphitheatre.
1938–42	Military facilities established in the Denver area include the Army Air Corps Technical School at Lowry Field, Rocky Mountain Arsenal, Buckley Field, and Remington Arms Plant, which later becomes the Denver Federal Center.
1947–55	Mayor James Quigg Newton modernizes Denver. Newton's traffic director, Henry A. Barnes, initiates one-way streets and "the Barnes Dance" (diagonal pedestrian crossings downtown).
1952	Colorado's first TV station, KFEL (Channel 2) in Denver, begins broadcasting.
	Inspired by watching television in a bar, Bill Daniels launches a cable television network. His and other cable companies' networks make the Denver area America's cable capital.

1953	The Rocky Flats facility to make plutonium "triggers" for hydrogen bombs begins operation northwest of Denver.
	Denver's first major shopping center, Cherry Creek, at First Avenue and University Boulevard, opens.
1955	The Glenn L. Martin Company builds a factory in Waterton Canyon, southwest of Denver, to make Titan missiles, leading to the metropolitan area becoming an aerospace hub.
1960	The Denver Broncos, the state's first major-league sports team, begin play.
	Corruption in the Denver Police Department comes to public attention. Eventually, more than fifty policemen are indicted for crimes such as burglary.
1962	The Denver Technological Center opens southeast of Denver, drawing population and business activity from the central city.
1965	Dana Crawford & Associates establish Larimer Square, sparking historic preservation that revives downtown Denver.
	The South Platte River floods on June 16. The disaster prompts construction of Chatfield Dam and inspires the creation of waterfront greenways.
	Metropolitan State College (later Metropolitan State University of Denver) holds its first classes on October 4, 1965, in rented facilities.
1966	Rodolfo "Corky" Gonzales founds Crusade for Justice to secure Chicano rights.
1967	Homestake Dam completed as part of a joint effort by Aurora and Colorado Springs to bring western Colorado water to those cities.
1969	The Rachel Noel Resolution calls for integration of Denver schools.
	Fire at Rocky Flats threatens to blanket the metropolitan area with deadly plutonium dust.
	Jefferson City incorporates to the west of Denver. It soon changes its name to Lakewood.
1970	Colorado wins the right to host the 1976 Winter Olympics in Denver and mountain towns, but in 1972 voters shun the opportunity by rejecting a tax increase to fund Olympic infrastructure.
	The US Census shows more people in the Denver metropolitan area living outside the Denver city limits than inside. In 2010 more

than 75 percent of people in the metropolitan area were living outside Denver.

1974   The Poundstone Amendment to the Colorado Constitution makes it difficult for Denver to annex territory.

1976   The Auraria Higher Education Center opens as a shared campus of the Community College of Denver, Metropolitan State University of Denver, and the University of Colorado Denver.

1978   The Denver Center for the Performing Arts opens as the nation's third-largest venue for theater, music, dance, and drama.

1982   The decline in the price of oil derails the economy.

1983   Federico F. Peña elected Denver's first Hispanic mayor.

1991   Wellington Edward Webb becomes the city's first African American mayor.

        Casino gambling begins in Black Hawk, Central City, and Cripple Creek, with part of the tax revenues supporting historic preservation.

1993   The Colorado Rockies, a Major League Baseball team, begin play in Denver.

        World Youth Day (August 11–16) and Pope John Paul II attract 186,000 pilgrims from throughout the world to Denver.

1994   The Regional Transportation District opens its first light-rail line from Broadway to Auraria to Five Points.

1995   Denver International Airport opens after costly delays.

1996   The Colorado Avalanche hockey team wins the Stanley Cup. It does so again in 2001.

1997   Summit of Eight world leaders meet in Denver, June 19–22.

1998–99 The Denver Broncos win consecutive Super Bowl championships.

1999   On April 20 two students murder twelve other students and one teacher at Columbine High School in Jefferson County.

2001   Colorado's sixty-fourth county, the City and County of Broomfield, begins operating.

2002   Wildfires, including the 137,000-acre Hayman fire, southwest of Denver, destroy hundreds of thousands of acres and kill nine people during a year of severe drought.

2003   John W. Hickenlooper Jr., a founder of Colorado's first brewpub, is elected mayor of Denver and, in 2010, governor of Colorado.

2004–8	The University of Colorado moves its health sciences center from Denver to Aurora, where the Anschutz Medical Campus takes shape on the grounds of the Fitzsimons Army Hospital, which closed in the late 1990s.
2008	The Democratic National Convention meets in Denver to nominate Barack Obama for president.
2009	After nearly 150 years, the *Rocky Mountain News,* Denver's first newspaper, ceases publishing.
2012	Aurora theater massacre on July 20 leaves twelve dead and seventy injured. In August 2015, the mentally ill shooter, James Holmes, was convicted of numerous homicides and other crimes and sentenced to numerous life terms in prison.
	Swimmer Missy (Melissa) Franklin of Centennial wins four gold medals and one bronze at the London Olympics.
2013	Boulder and other towns north of Denver suffer from floods.
2014	Private recreational use of marijuana for those over twenty-one legalized under state law as a result of a 2012 amendment to the Colorado Constitution. Denver becomes the state's pot hub.
2015	Voters approve commercial development of land around Denver International Airport and redevelopment of the National Western Stock Show complex and its environs.
2016	Denver Broncos defeat Carolina Panthers, 24–10, to win Super Bowl 50. In March star quarterback Peyton Manning announces his retirement.
2016	Regional Transportation District opens Vail lines to Denver International Airport, Arvada Westminister and Wheat Ridge.

A Short History of Denver

Chapter One

From Camping Grounds to Towns

uring the past three hundred million years, the Denver metropolitan area has been under water and above water, higher and lower than it is now, warmer and colder. It has been home to dinosaurs and mammoths, bison, elk, antelope, and an ark full of other species, including humans. It has witnessed mountains rise and fall, with the current Rockies coming into their glory after crustal upheavals that began some sixty-seven million years ago.

Over the eons, debris deposited by swamps, seas, and eroding mountains created thousands of feet of sedimentary rock now buried under the city. Near the base of the mountains, subterranean forces tilted those layers upward to create hogbacks and sandstone formations such as the Dakota Hogback, where footprints of three-toed dinosaurs may be seen. Crustal movements also thrust up the jutting slabs in Red Rocks, Roxborough Park, and the Flatirons. Among these monoliths, archaeologists have found the area's oldest homes—rock shelters. Archaic era (5500 BCE–0) peoples built these residences tucked into the nooks and crannies of rock. They left behind the stone tools used to kill and butcher game. Bone hooks and net sinkers show they fished. Spear throwers and projectile points prove they hunted. Even earlier, between 10,000 and 8000 BCE, Clovis and Folsom peoples traversed the base of the mountains.

Native Americans favored the region because of its fortunate location, with access to the plains and the mountains. Lying in a trough along the eastern base of the Front Range, a subdivision of the Southern Rockies, Denver's site is more sheltered than the high plains to the east and often cooler in summer and warmer in winter than higher land to the west, east, and south. The city's main waterway, the South Platte

River, tumbles out of the mountains through picturesque Waterton Canyon, about twenty-five miles south of downtown. Captured and channeled by the trough, the river flows through southern suburbs, including Littleton and Englewood, and into the heart of the city, where it meets Cherry Creek, which drains high land to the southeast. North of the city limits, the South Platte intersects other streams, such as Clear and Ralston Creeks, which contribute mountain water. Then the river slants northeastward on its way to irrigate farms in northeastern Colorado. In Nebraska it joins the North Platte to form the Platte, a tributary of the Missouri River, which in turn empties into the Mississippi. Along those watercourses Native Americans found water, shade, and in the winter sheltered camping sites. When warmer weather arrived, they spread out onto the plains to pursue bison and in high summer followed the animals into vast mountain valleys, such as South, Middle, and North Parks.

For centuries, the first beneficiaries of the area's favored location enjoyed much of what they wanted and needed. They were only sporadically bothered by Spanish and French claimants to what became Colorado because neither France nor Spain effectively occupied the area. What the Indians did not have, a piece of parchment sealed with blobs of red wax, foreshadowed their undoing. That document, the 1803 Louisiana Purchase, gave the United States a claim to the land. France got fifteen million dollars, and the United States got more than 800,000 square miles, mostly made up of the western drainage basin of the Mississippi River. For the 153 square miles that today constitute the City and County of Denver, a flyspeck on the huge map of Louisiana, the United States paid less than three thousand dollars. The French left behind a few place-names, including Platte, which means "flat."

Arapaho and Cheyenne

The Southern Arapaho (Hinono'eino) and Southern Cheyenne (Tsitsistas), allied tribes that in 1800 occupied the northeastern part of what would one day be called Colorado, initially had little reason to worry about a real estate deal made in Paris. Except for a few traders and trappers, Euro-Americans were not interested in the dry plains north of the Arkansas River, tracts that many, including US explorer Stephen H. Long, who visited the area in 1820, considered a desert. To eastern and midwestern farmers, the Platte River country seemed nearly worthless and hence a good place for Indians. At times the Arapaho camped along Cherry Creek, near its junction with the South Platte River, naming the creek for the wild chokecherries they harvested along its banks. Their fondness for that waterway led St. Louis fur trader Auguste P. Chouteau in 1815 to host a trading camp there, where he bartered with the Indians for buffalo robes, beaver pelts, and wild horses.

The name *Arapaho* may have come from the Pawnee word for "buyer" or "trader." They called themselves "bison path people" or "our people." Others referred to them as the "Tattooed People," because they scratched their breasts with a yucca-leaf needle and then rubbed wood ashes into the wound to make an indelible mark. They arrived in Colorado around 1800, pushed from their Great Lakes homelands by other tribes. After crossing the Missouri River, the Arapaho split. The northern branch headed for what would become Wyoming, the southern offshoot for Colorado. As they lapped against the eastern edge of the Southern Rockies, they met resistance from the Ute. Consequently, the Arapaho lodged at the base of the Front Range, with as many as fifteen hundred camping on the future site of Denver in the 1840s and 1850s.

The Cheyenne, as historian Elliot West tells in *The Contested Plains: Indians, Goldseekers, and the Rush to Colorado* (1998), also left their ancestral homes. Obtaining horses, they became superb riders and expert bison hunters. For them and for the Arapaho, bison were the animal equivalent of gold—the mother lode that undergirded their economies and shaped their societies. In 1851, by terms of the Treaty of Fort Laramie, the United States promised both tribes that they could continue hunting between the Arkansas and North Platte Rivers. Just seven years later, in 1858, the promise crumbled when newcomers discovered the metallic gold they craved in the sands of the South Platte.

Gold and Wars, 1858–1869

The forces that gave the Native Americans a pleasant home also created conditions that, coupled with other factors such as disease and the decline of the bison herds, hastened the Indians' demise. Less than forty miles west of Denver are Front Range mountains interlaced in a few places with a heavy yellow metal savagely coveted by Euro-Americans willing to risk their own lives and kill others to get it. Millions of years of erosion scattered grains of that gold at the base of the Rockies, where in midsummer 1858 prospectors recovered some of it from South Platte placer deposits. News of those strikes raced eastward, prompting hundreds of gold seekers (sometimes called Argonauts, in reference to the tale from Greek mythology of Jason and his Argonauts, who sought the Golden Fleece in a ship named *Argo*).

In 1859 the Argonaut trickle turned into a flood. Pursuing their dreams of securing a good living, some of them hoped to add to their wealth. Others came out of desperation born of an economic depression that began in the late 1850s. Part of a long-term westward movement, many considered it their destiny to occupy the continent. In some ways, the newcomers, most of them young men, were similar to the Native Americans. Both were pushed and pulled by economic forces. The differences were also obvious. The Euro-Americans, unlike most of the Indians, wanted to mine, ranch, and farm; to construct railroads; and to make cities. In their world there was little, if any, room or hope for the bison or for the Native Americans.

At first, the Tattooed People, who had traded with whites for decades and whose daughters had sometimes married Euro-American fur traders, welcomed the "spider people," the name the Arapaho gave the whites. Chief Little Raven entertained them in his handsomely decorated teepee and visited with them in their log cabins. Arapaho friendliness is demonstrated by the saga of the Blue brothers, Alexander, Daniel, and Charles. The Blues ran out of food as they journeyed west in the spring of 1859. After Alexander and Charles died, Daniel survived by eating their remains. He too might have starved had it not been for an Arapaho who found him, fed him, and brought him to Denver, where townsfolk scraped together enough money to send him back to Illinois. Unlike the Blues, most pilgrims arrived safely at Auraria and Denver, the towns that sprouted in the autumn of 1858 along Cherry Creek, near its confluence with the South Platte. By the spring of 1859, the Arapaho and Cheyenne had been swamped by energetic, well-armed aliens, many of whom regarded Indians as degraded people.

Many of the interlopers, finding little gold, quickly gave up and, like Daniel Blue, went home. Others followed the lure of gold into the

Little Raven, head chief of the Southern Arapaho, offered hospitality to the white fortune seekers in 1859. His generosity was poorly repaid in 1864 at the Sand Creek Massacre. Courtesy Denver Public Library.

mountains. Unfortunately for the Indians, a few thousand whites recognized that they could make money in the supply towns at the base of the mountains. By 1860 around five thousand people were ensconced in Denver and Auraria on land the Treaty of Fort Laramie had promised to the Cheyenne and the Arapaho. To provide legal cover for their citizens' land grab, the US government in the fall of 1860 invited the Cheyenne and Arapaho to meet with federal agents, including Albert Gallatin Boone, grandson of frontiersman Daniel Boone, at Fort Wise (later renamed Fort Lyon), on the Arkansas River, more than 160 miles southeast of Denver. Negotiations dragged on for months. Finally, early in 1861, ten Cheyenne and Arapaho chiefs, including Little Raven, signed the Treaty of Fort Wise. Other tribesmen objected. George Bird Grinnell in his *The Fighting Cheyennes* (1956) recounts that some Arapaho complained that "they had not been present [at the treaty signing] and had received nothing for their 'land and their gold.'" Little Raven, Grinnell reports, remembered, "The Cheyennes signed [the Treaty of Fort Wise] first, then I; but we did not know what it was. That is one reason why I want an interpreter, so I can know what I sign." Whites, on the other hand, liked the treaty because it erased the claims of the Native Americans to most of northeastern Colorado, including the Denver area.

Losing land was bad enough, but the two tribes' problems ran even deeper. For more than a decade, the bison herds upon which they had depended had been declining. The Indians' huge horse herds overgrazed the grasslands, and Euro-American migrations to Utah, Washington, Oregon, and California further stressed the plains ecosystem. By the early 1860s, many of the Indians were starving and sometimes raided ranches on the plains looking for food. In June 1864, four young Arapaho killed Nathan Hungate; his wife, Ellen; and their two young daughters on a ranch near Elizabeth, 25 miles southeast of Denver. People gaped at the Hungates' bullet-riddled bodies paraded naked through town in an ox wagon, vowed vengeance, and grew fearful. In July, seeing a cloud of dust south of town, citizens convinced themselves that Indians were about to attack. Women and children fled to stout brick buildings, where they remained until scouts reported that the dust had been stirred up by peaceful freighters.

Colorado's territorial governor John Evans capitalized on the Hungates' deaths to convince the federal government to pay volunteer troops to control the Native Americans. Peace chiefs, including Black Kettle of the Cheyenne, risked their lives by coming to hostile Denver in mid-September 1864 to meet with Evans and Colonel John Milton Chivington, the district military commander, at Camp Weld, a mile south of town near the intersection of today's West Eighth Avenue and Vallejo Street. Evans weaseled out of the conversation by saying that he was not a military authority. Chivington also parsed his words. While saying that he was "not a big war chief," he also declared that all the soldiers in the region were under his command. He indicated that as long as Black Kettle and his people maintained good relations with Major Edward W. Wynkoop at Fort Lyon on the Arkansas River, there would not be war. Black Kettle returned to Fort Lyon, where he and other Cheyenne and Arapaho stayed until Wynkoop was removed from command and a new post commander told the Indians to leave. They went north to camp on Sand Creek. There Chivington mounted a sneak attack at dawn on November 29, 1864. Despite the Indians' attempts to signal that they were peaceful, soldiers continued to fire. By day's end at least 163 Indians, mostly Cheyenne, many of them women and children, had been slaughtered. Souvenir-hunting troops hacked off parts of the Indians' bodies as trophies.

The US House of Representatives' Committee on the Conduct of the War concluded in 1865 that Chivington had committed a "foul and dastardly massacre." In Denver, where an army board took testimony, many people sided with Chivington. One who did not, Captain Silas Soule, who had refused to participate in the bloodbath, courageously testified against the colonel. For that the captain was killed by an assassin who got away. In *Bury My Heart at Wounded Knee,* Dee Brown quotes Little Raven's lament: "That fool band of soldiers cleared out our lodges, and killed our women and children . . . at Sand Creek. . . . Left Hand, White Antelope and many chiefs lie there, and our horses were taken from us there. . . . Our friends are buried there, and we hate to leave these grounds."

In reprisal for Sand Creek, some Native Americans raided plains settlements and attacked wagon trains in 1865, but Little Raven and Black Kettle kept pressing for peace. Treaties in 1865 (Little Arkansas) and 1868 (Medicine Lodge) and the 1869 battle of Summit Springs in northeastern Colorado led to the removal of the Cheyenne and Arapaho from Colorado. Many were banished to Indian Territory, which later became Oklahoma. Black Kettle was killed there in 1869 at the Washita Massacre, and Little Raven died a natural death there in 1889. Later, some of the Southern Cheyenne joined their kin in Wyoming. In an 1884 interview preserved at the University of California's Bancroft Library, John Evans argued, "The benefit to Colorado of that massacre, as they call it, was very great for it ridded the plains of the indians [*sic*]." His view reflected his and most other Euro-Americans' conviction that clearing the region of Indians was necessary for Denver's survival. It also mirrored his bank account. He and other empire builders snatched up land that had belonged to the Arapaho and Cheyenne and pocketed the profits as the city grew. A little more than 150 years after the massacre, Colorado governor John Hickenlooper Jr. formally apologized.

Town Founding

Hickenlooper's apology did not change the map. To the victors belonged the spoils—much of Colorado, including Denver. It was a city, like many others, founded by those who hoped to make a better life for themselves, perhaps even to get rich. What better to attract wealth seekers than gold?

Reports of glittering riches had floated out of the Rockies and the Southwest for centuries. On June 22, 1850, Cherokee Indians on their way to California's goldfields made a well-documented gold find on Ralston's Creek, near Fifty-Sixth Avenue and Fenton Street in present-day Arvada, but the small strike did not cause them to tarry. Seven years later, Hispanic prospectors panned in the South Platte River, near what is today Florida Avenue, and in the same year a small party of Missourians said they had found gold in the area.

But it was not until 1858 that reports proved alluring enough to trigger a massive gold rush. That summer William Greeneberry "Green" Russell, a seasoned gold seeker from Georgia, led a party of prospectors, including his brothers, Levi and Joseph, to the South Platte River in western Kansas Territory. There in mid-July they found a respectable placer deposit, gold flakes mixed with river sand, where Little Dry Creek enters the river near Dartmouth Avenue and Santa Fe Drive in present-day Englewood. A few weeks later, another group from Lawrence, Kansas, panned more South Platte gold from near the Russells' site. Together the finds probably amounted to less than 150 ounces, but from modest discoveries great hopes blossomed. As news of the finds, accompanied by goose quills packed with gold dust, spread east, other gamblers risked their lives by trekking more than six hundred miles from eastern Kansas and Nebraska to what they called Pikes Peak country, imprecisely named for the mountain seventy miles to the south of the South Platte discoveries.

Auraria

The fortune seekers hoped to find gold, but some also banked on cashing in on gold fever by grabbing land, founding towns, and selling lots. With a keen eye for prime real estate, the Russell party established their town, Auraria, on the southwestern side of Cherry Creek, near its juncture with the South Platte. Auraria borrowed its name from the Russells' hometown in northern Georgia. There in the early 1830s the most important gold strikes in the eastern United States had catalyzed Georgians into driving many of the Cherokee Indians out of that region. The list of stockholders in the Auraria Town Company dated November 1, 1858, included Joseph and William Greeneberry Russell, both of whom had

scampered back to the warmer East, telling golden tales as they traveled. Remaining Aurarians, not sure what a winter at the base of snowcapped mountains might bring, set to work building log cabins chinked with mud.

The tent town of Auraria quickly evolved into a log-and-frame community. Denver, a larger town on the other side of Cherry Creek, created a month after Auraria, soon annexed the smaller town. Courtesy *Frank Leslie's Illustrated Newspaper*, August 20, 1859.

Heading the Auraria stockholders' list was William McGaa, a trader and trapper whom the founders courted because he had several Indian wives and hence could provide cover for their taking Indian land. They named a street for McGaa, a fleeting tribute that by the late 1860s had been changed by officials who no longer needed McGaa and who considered a polygamist with a fondness for whiskey unfit to associate with less pickled citizens, some of whom, although they approved of defrauding Native Americans, attended church on Sunday. For decades, similarly minded people refused to count McGaa's son, William Denver, born in March 1859, as the first baby born in the Cherry Creek settlements. They preferred to give the honor to Auraria Humbell, born in July in Auraria, or to John Denver Stout, born in August in Denver. Both of them, as far as anyone knew, had properly wed, monogamous non-Indian parents. A couple of months before McGaa joined the Auraria

Town Company, he and a few others had staked out a town venture on the northeastern side of Cherry Creek, near Fifteenth and Blake Streets, a better location than Auraria because much of it was on higher ground and near an Indian and trapper path, known as the Smoky Hill or Cherokee Trail, which ran a few hundred feet north of Cherry Creek, roughly along the route of today's Fifteenth Street. McGaa and his friends called their would-be metropolis St. Charles, but because they did little to develop or protect it, they soon found themselves outmaneuvered by William H. Larimer Jr.

William H. Larimer Jr.

The forty-nine-year-old Larimer was typical of a subset of westerners of the mid-1800s, an energetic breed of dream-big, get-rich-quick, take-giant-risks entrepreneurs. Accompanied by others, including his seventeen-year-old son, William H. H., he left Leavenworth in eastern Kansas in mid-October and arrived in Auraria in mid-November. Grasping the merits of the St. Charles site, Larimer seized it on November 22, 1858, staking his claim by crossing four cottonwood logs near the southwestern corner of what became Fifteenth and Larimer Streets and building a small cabin there. Probably sensing that he might need the favor of Kansas officials when it came time to establish the legitimacy of his claim, Larimer named his village Denver City, for James W. Denver, the man he supposed to be governor of Kansas Territory. Actually, Denver, a former newspaper editor and a duelist who had killed a man in California, had been governor of Kansas when Larimer left Leavenworth, but he had resigned while Larimer was working his way west. Samuel Medary, Denver's successor, was really governor, but Larimer did not know it, so today the Denver Broncos are not the Medary Broncos and singer-songwriter John Denver (born Henry John Deutschendorf Jr.) did not become John Medary.

In a letter to the wife and eight children whom he had left behind in Leavenworth, Larimer wrote, "It is well the Pilgrims landed upon Plymouth Rock and settled up that country before they saw this one or that would now remain unsettled. Everyone will soon be flocking to Denver for the most picturesque country in the world, with fine air, good

William H. Larimer, Jr. founded Denver City on November 22, 1858, only to abandon his struggling town five years later. Courtesy History Colorado.

water, and everything to make man happy and live to a good old age." He boasted, "I am Denver City."

Knowing that transportation links would be the key to survival for his isolated "city," Larimer gave the Leavenworth and Pike's Peak Express Company fifty-three town lots and shares in the town company to persuade it to locate in Denver rather than Auraria. On May 7, 1859, the first two stages rumbled into town. By securing the stagecoach connections to the Missouri Valley towns, Larimer doomed Auraria and other rivals. Passengers left from and arrived in Denver, as did the mail, which had to be picked up at the stage office. Hotels and restaurants wanted to be near the stage terminus. In late 1859 Auraria admitted defeat and merged into Denver, losing its original name and becoming known as West Denver. Consolidating the towns made sense because by the end of 1859, both were feeling pinched as the gold rush lost its steam.

Perhaps as many as a hundred thousand Argonauts crossed the plains in 1859. Few could afford stagecoach fares, so most walked or slowly trundled along in ox-drawn wagons. Their hopes rose as they approached Denver and fell as soon as they realized that the gold in Cherry Creek and the South Platte was too scarce and widely distributed to sustain more than a lucky few. Briefly, real estate values skyrocketed. Then

HOLLADAY OVERLAND MAIL & EXPRESS CO.

Stagecoach king Ben Holladay bought the Leavenworth and Pike's Peak Express Company and its stage station at Fifteenth and Market Streets in 1862. Grateful Denverites renamed McGaa Street Holladay Street. After that street became the city's red-light district, the name was changed in 1887 to Market Street. Courtesy History Colorado.

the bubble burst and prices plummeted. Fortunately, rich placer and lode gold discoveries in mountains less than fifty miles from Denver saved the city, which survived as a supply, service, processing, and to some degree manufacturing center.

Larimer's town struggled in the early 1860s, but he stuck around for a few years. His proposed town of Highland, north of Denver across the South Platte, did not take root until others developed it as Highlands more than a decade later. His other major undertaking, Mount Prospect, Denver's first cemetery, which he and his son established on a hill a couple of miles southeast of town in 1861, gradually filled up with corpses, some victims of the violence that marked the area's rough first years. Larimer too might have lingered long enough to occupy his boneyard had he gotten the jobs he wanted. Early in 1861, the US Congress carved out chunks of Nebraska, Kansas, New Mexico, and Utah Territories to form Colorado Territory. As the founder of Denver City, Larimer reckoned he had a good chance to be appointed the first governor. He traveled to Washington, DC, to lobby the incoming president, Abraham Lincoln, for the position, only to see William Gilpin get the job in March 1861. Then Larimer ran for mayor, but as a crusty middle-aged Presbyterian he proved unpopular with the town's young, largely male, and often carousing population.

Decrying Denver's "lack of comforts," Larimer returned to Leavenworth in 1862 and later became a Union captain in the Civil War. After the war he farmed in Leavenworth, where he died at age sixty-five in 1875. Green Russell also left Colorado, and true to his Georgia heritage he supported the Confederacy. He died at age fifty-nine in Indian Territory in 1877. Like many of the Fifty-Eighters and Fifty-Niners who gave up and left too soon, Russell and Larimer let others reap what they had sown.

Reminders

Place-name and other reminders of the Arapaho and Cheyenne remain today. Skyscrapers dot Arapahoe Street in downtown Denver, and Little Raven Street connects Speer Boulevard with Twentieth Street. In the suburb of Westminster, near West 104th Avenue and Westminster Boulevard, Little Raven has been memorialized in bronze by sculptress Marie Barbera. In Arapahoe County, officials dedicated Cheyenne/Arapaho Park on June 7, 1996, at 9300 East Iowa Avenue. Wildflowers frame this park, which contains a ceremonial Native American circle, red sandstone slabs inscribed with Indian memories, and an abstracted lodgepole and I-beam sculpture. Also in Aurora at the University of Colorado's Anschutz Medical Campus, the Nighthorse Campbell Native Health Building, completed in 2002, architecturally reflects Indian tepees, kivas, and shade shelters and recognizes former US senator Ben Nighthorse Campbell, a member of the Northern Cheyenne tribe who did much to ensure that the Sand Creek Massacre site would be dedicated as a National Historic Site in 2007. The University of Colorado–Boulder's decision to name dormitories Chief Left Hand and Chief Niwot, rather than use Indian names, stirred controversy in 2014. Left Hand's Arapaho name is commonly incorrectly rendered as Niwot but is actually Nowoo3. Little Raven is commonly given as Hosa but is actually Houusoo. After some wrangling, the university agreed to use these Indian names.

Take a stroll in and around Civic Center Park in the heart of Denver to learn about the city's Native American heritage. Start two blocks south of the park at East Twelfth Avenue and Broadway to visit the History Colorado Museum, where displays often feature Colorado's Indian patrimony. Walk north a block to the Denver Public Library at West Thirteenth Avenue and Broadway and ask a librarian in the Western History and Genealogy Department to show you an original copy of the US House of Representatives' 1865 report that condemned Chivington. From the library walk east on East Fourteenth Avenue to the east side of the state capitol to view Preston Powers's bronze statue *The Closing Era*, which, true to the nineteenth-century view that Native Americans were fated to vanish, depicts the intertwined demise of the Indians and the bison. Donors wanted to place the statue on the prominent west side of the capitol, but, as historian Derek Everett explains in his book *The Colorado State Capitol: History, Politics, Preservation* (2005), anti-Indian sentiment in the 1890s prevented them from doing so.

Loop around to the west side of the capitol to look at the base of the 1909 monument to the Civil War dead. There you will see the name of Silas Soule, shot down because he stood up for the Indians. The monument refers to a "battle" at Sand Creek rather than a massacre. In 1999 the Colorado General Assembly authorized an additional plaque that explained: "By designating Sand Creek a battle, the monument's designers mischaracterized the actual events. Protests led by some Sand Creek descendants and others throughout the twentieth century have since led to the widespread recognition of the tragedy as the Sand Creek Massacre."

Walk northwest to the triangular plot at the intersection of West Colfax and Broadway, where Frederick MacMonnies proposed to sculpt a memorial honoring Indians, but city fathers decided instead to praise frontier scout Christopher "Kit" Carson, who tops the monument dedicated in 1911. Then glance down at the few feet of rutted asphalt known as Cheyenne Place, one of the city's shortest and least known streets, at the western edge of the triangle.

Cross Cheyenne Place and enter Civic Center Park. Consider what percentage of the homeless people lingering there might be Native Americans whose ancestors called all of northeastern Colorado home before 1861. Pause before the statue of Christopher Columbus, often the focal point for protesting Indians who wish he had never sailed the ocean blue. Take a look at Alexander Phimister Proctor's 1922 statue *On the Warpath,* a bronze rendering of the romantic view of Indians many Euro-Americans adopted after Native Americans were exiled. Go south from the park to the Denver Art Museum to see selections from their renowned collection of Native art. Tarry a few minutes at the northeastern corner of the fortress-like Ponti-Sudler building to view the ten stylized red metal trees created by Edgar Heap of Birds, an Arapaho-Cheyenne artist. Read the inscriptions: "Bison Life Ends Rez Life Begins 160 Acres Plow and Poverty" and "Gold Wars Starve Suffer." On a semicircular wall behind the little grove, gray letters proclaim NAH-KEV-HO-EYEA-ZIM, "We are always returning home again." Near the ground a small sign, not part of the art assembly, informs homeless people, including Native Americans, that a city ordinance prohibits them from sheltering there between 10:00 p.m. and 6:00 a.m. Police will expel them as their ancestors were expelled more than 150 years ago.

Chapter Two

City Building, 1859–1876

*D*enver's high hopes born of the 1859 gold rush soon faded, as prospectors flocked to the mountains or gave up and returned home. The fledgling town survived as a supply, service, government, and transportation center, but in the 1860s, beset by fire, flood, isolation, Indian threats, and the Civil War, it stagnated. In an entire decade it added only 10 people to its population, reaching 4,759 in 1870. Thanks to railroad connections and improvements in Colorado's economy, the town blossomed in the early 1870s. By 1876, when Colorado shed its territorial status and became a state, Denver was its dominant city, with around 24,000 people. Seen through the life and work of William Newton Byers, founder and publisher of the *Rocky Mountain News,* the town's first newspaper, the skeleton chronicle takes on flesh, blood, and a little scandal.

Byers: Booster Extraordinaire

In early 1859, William Newton Byers joined William H. Larimer Jr. as one of Denver's chief boosters. Born in Ohio in 1831, Byers worked as a land surveyor in Iowa, Oregon, Washington, and Nebraska, where in the 1850s he dabbled in Omaha politics. Seeing an opportunity to cash in on the 1859 gold rush, he hauled a printing press from Omaha to Auraria. Late on the evening of April 22, 1859, assisted by Jack Smith, an African American who manned the press, Byers published the first issue of the *Rocky Mountain News,* which he dated April 23, 1859. He soon signaled his intention to remain by fetching his wife, Elizabeth, and his two small children, Mary and Frank, to join him. For nearly twenty years, Byers used the *News* to champion railroad construction, mining, manufacturing, agriculture, tourism, and statehood for Colorado. Sometimes he

William Newton Byers founded the *Rocky Mountain News* (1859–2009) and became Denver's greatest booster. Courtesy Tom Noel Collection.

stretched the truth, as he did on September 10, 1859, when he launched a "Boat Departures" column: "'Ute' and 'Cheyenne' for mouth of the Platte. Scow 'Arapahoe' for New Orleans." That, local people knew, was a joke because the South Platte was rarely navigable even for small boats. Byers wanted to sell newspapers, so he fed his readers humor as well as the crime, disaster, political, business, and scandal stories they wanted to read.

Crime

Even though Byers knew that crime reports sold newspapers, he hated crime. A ruffian had blasted him with a shotgun in Omaha. In the Cherry Creek settlements, things were not any better. At first he housed the *Rocky Mountain News* in the attic of Richens Wootton's saloon in Auraria. Drunks on the first floor enjoyed shooting their pistols into the ceiling. Byers and his staff did not enjoy dancing around bullets, so they laid down metal sheeting to deflect the blasts from below. When a year later, on July 18, 1860, the *News* lambasted "the rowdies, ruffians, shoulder-hitters and bullies generally, that infest our city," one of the bullies shot up the *News* office, and later some of them kidnapped Byers and might have killed him had not a sensible saloon keeper saved him.

Vigilantes and people's courts lynched at least a dozen people in Denver and its environs during the nineteenth century. After hangings, bodies were sometimes left dangling as a warning to other criminals. Courtesy Tom Noel Collection.

From April 1859 until December 1860, the *News* chronicled at least six murders, five hangings ordered by the people's courts, and at least three lynchings of suspected miscreants by vigilantes. During the Civil War, the community grew more peaceful, but after the war crime flared again. Perhaps as many as fifteen men were lynched near or in Denver between 1866 and 1868, including L. H. Musgrove, accused of robbery and of being friendly to Indians, hanged from the Larimer Street Bridge across Cherry Creek on November 22, 1868.

Fire and Flood

The town was hastily built, mainly of wood. In a time of candles, kerosene lamps, and wood-burning stoves, fire was both friend and foe. Byers's home burned in October 1860, nearly killing his son. Concerned citizens discussed establishing a volunteer fire department but dillydallied. When a fire broke out near Fifteenth and Blake Streets on April 19, 1863, the response, which included tearing down buildings in the inferno's path, was ineffective, and much of the business district was incinerated by the wind-driven flames. Boys profited by sifting through the rubble for reusable nails, and a new and sturdier town, much of it made from brick, rose from the ashes.

A little more than a year later, Mother Nature taught Denverites that even brick structures were subject to her whims. On May 20, 1864, Cherry Creek floodwaters swept away buildings, doing even more damage than the 1863 fire. Indians had warned settlers not to build in the creek bed, but the pioneers, who rarely saw much water in the sandy channel, coveted the land as prime real estate. Byers housed his newspaper office in a frame structure that stood on stilts, which allowed water to flow under it until the flood smashed it and washed its three-thousand-pound press away. John Dailey, Byers's partner, and several employees, who were sleeping in the building, survived. Probably twenty or more citizens did not. Property damage was estimated at $350,000, a huge sum at the time. Byers and his family were living on a ranch on the banks of the South Platte. As the swollen river lapped at their feet, he crammed a note in a bottle to alert would-be rescuers. Soldiers under the command of Colonel John M. Chivington saved Byers, and territorial governor John Evans gave the editor and his family temporary shelter in the governor's home.

Empire Builders

That Evans would welcome Byers made sense because they were kindred spirits and political allies. The governor, a medical doctor, developed the Chicago suburb of Evanston in the 1850s and helped found Northwestern University there. When William Gilpin was forced to resign as territorial governor in 1862 for making unauthorized expenditures, Evans snatched the job. He showed that he was more than a fly-by-night politician by bringing his wife, Margaret, west in late 1862. They traveled by stage, covering the six hundred miles from Atchison, Kansas, to Denver in a little less than a week because Evans ordered the coach to run day and night. After the scandal of the 1864 Sand Creek Massacre, Evans was forced to resign the governorship, but he remained a powerful figure in Denver until his death in 1897.

Like Byers, Evans staked his career and his fortune, which was considerably larger than Byers's, on the city's success, which, in turn,

John Evans, noted for bringing railroads to Denver and championing education, was removed as territorial governor in the wake of the Sand Creek Massacre, a stain on Colorado he might have prevented. Courtesy History Colorado, painting by Waldo Love.

depended upon Colorado's success. They touted the territory's agricultural potential and rejoiced when farming settlements such as Union Colony (Greeley), Longmont, and Fort Collins, all north of Denver, cropped up in the early 1870s. Similarly, they celebrated new mining strikes and the technical advances that allowed smelters to unlock the gold and silver wealth bound up in the Rockies' ores. Several times in the 1860s, they unsuccessfully campaigned to get Colorado made a state. They failed in 1864 in part because Hispanic residents in southern Colorado did not trust the Evans-Byers crowd in Denver. Their efforts in 1865 also came to nothing because the proposed state constitution denied African Americans the right to vote, a denial of civil rights that local blacks decried. Finally, in 1876, they celebrated statehood. Five years later, in 1881, Denver won permanent designation as Colorado's capital, having filled that role in the 1870s on a temporary basis.

Railroads, Byers and Evans knew, were critical to the city's success. Freighting goods more than five hundred miles across the plains by slow ox-drawn wagons burdened Coloradans with exorbitant transportation costs for everything they imported or exported. Few visitors were willing to pay high fares and spend a bone-jarring week or more in a cramped stagecoach to reach Denver. Only those with pressing business, the adventuresome, healthy, and unrushed, had the motivation, time, and stamina it took to get to Colorado.

John Nicolay, President Abraham Lincoln's private secretary, spent twelve days (including time off to hunt bison) to reach Denver from Atchison in 1863. An August 17, 1863, letter he wrote to his friend John Hay preserved in the Nicolay Papers at the Library of Congress gives a hint of his experience riding in a hot, dusty coach with six passengers, an African American baby, and a lot of baggage: "I leave your own imagination to picture the comforts and delights of a 78 hours ride [from Fort Kearney, Nebraska, where Nicolay ended his bison hunt] through a desert in August.... Yet I still live." To reach Central City, 45 miles from Denver, Nicolay traveled by buggy. Leaving in the afternoon, he journeyed 25 miles in eight hours before stopping at the Michigan House, a wayside inn in Golden Gate Canyon, where he dined on apple pie and milk and slept on a hard bed. Leaving at dawn, he arrived in Central City the same day. In late September, Nicolay ventured south from Denver. It took him more than thirteen hours by stagecoach at an average speed of 5 miles an hour to reach Colorado City (now a part of Colorado Springs); another day to get to Pueblo; another to reach Sangre de Christo Pass, the gateway to the San Luis Valley; and yet another to reach Fort Garland—a four-day journey that, barring I-25 traffic jams, would today take five or six hours.

With their city's fortunes dependent on railroads, boosters suffered a potentially fatal blow in the mid-1860s when Union Pacific (UP) officials decided to leave Denver off their transcontinental rail line. They opted to build through Wyoming rather than through Colorado's high, rough, and snowy mountains. To save their city and their investments in it, Evans, Byers, druggist Walter Scott Cheesman, banker David H. Moffat, and others backed the Denver Pacific Railway to link with the Union Pacific in Cheyenne. Finding it difficult to raise local money, Evans put the Denver Pacific under the Union Pacific's control, which got him the funds he needed to lay 106 miles of track between Denver and Cheyenne by mid-1870. The same summer connections to the East via the Kansas Pacific gave Denver additional access to the outside world. Symbolically, as the Kansas Pacific, under the direction of William Jackson Palmer,

was chugging toward Denver from the east and the Denver Pacific was advancing north, the Cheyenne lost their last significant battle in Colorado at Summit Springs, southwest of Sterling, on July 11, 1869.

Over the next forty years, Evans, Palmer, and others extended railroads along the Front Range, deep into the mountains, and into the plateau country of western Colorado. Palmer's Denver and Rio Grande played a key role in Denver's development because it linked the city to Colorado Springs, a town Palmer created and near where he lived; to Pueblo, which became the state's second-largest city by 1890 (24,558 people compared to Denver's 106,713); and to numerous other places in Colorado, including Alamosa, Leadville, Aspen, Montrose, Ouray, Durango, and Grand Junction. Often eastern capitalists gained control of those lines, just as they had with the Denver Pacific, because local entrepreneurs, though rich in vision, energy, and swagger, were often short of capital. With railroads subservient to the wishes of eastern financiers, Denver suffered from high freight rates. But railroads were better than ox wagons lumbering along at less than 2 miles an hour, and it was greatly to the city's benefit to be at the center of a spiderweb of rails—a network encompassing nearly 4,300 miles of track within the state by 1890. By rapidly becoming Colorado's transportation hub, Denver secured its future as the state's most important city.

Scandal

As economic prospects brightened, Byers's future dimmed. By early 1876, Denver was booming and Colorado's statehood was looming. Rail connections drove prices down and brought tourists and settlers in. Why, then, did Byers dynamite himself in April 1876 by publishing the love letters he had exchanged with Hattie E. Sancomb, a divorcée with whom he had had a dalliance? When he tried to end the affair, the spurned Sancomb ineffectively shot at him with her pearl-handled pistol, while Elizabeth, his wife, looked on. Perhaps he could have hushed up his foolery, if some of Hattie's letters had not fallen into the hands of one of his rival editors, who tried to blackmail Byers. To foil the blackmailer, "Wandering Will" printed the mortifying story in his own newspaper. His fall from grace, some said, destroyed his chances of becoming Colorado's governor. He also suffered by exiting the newspaper business in 1878 when Denver was enjoying rapid growth that would make it the nation's twenty-sixth-largest city by 1890. He may have found some comfort in regaining enough respect to become president of the Colorado Historical Society in 1879 and by being selected to head the Chamber of Commerce in 1893.

Exits

Byers, who died in 1903, was buried at Fairmount Cemetery with all the funeral fanfare due a prominent pioneer. Nearby markers memorialize Elizabeth, who died in 1920; son Frank (d. 1937); and daughter Mary Robinson, who lived in Denver from age two in 1859 to her death in 1940. Byers Canyon, Byers Peak, the town of Byers, Byers Branch Library, Byers School, Byers Place, and a stained-glass window in the state capitol commemorate a man who recorded and made history.

John Evans was also honored as a pioneer and for his multifaceted role—among other accomplishments, he founded the University of Denver—in making Denver a civilized and significant city. He begat a dynasty, including sons William Gray and Evan, daughter Anne, and grandson John Evans, all of whom remained powerful long after his passing. A major Denver avenue, a street in Cheyenne, a town abutting Greeley, and, most important, Mount Evans, the most prominent peak directly west of Denver, keep his name alive, as does his tombstone at Riverside Cemetery. No longer, however, is he revered as he once was. His vision of civilization, which reckoned ridding the plains of Native Americans as a reasonable act, eventually sickened civilized people. At the University of Denver, which had lionized him for more than a century, a faculty group assessed his role in the Sand Creek Massacre and in November 2014 issued the *Report of the John Evans Study Committee,* which stated: "In effect, through his lobbying receipt of, and support for the 3rd Regiment, Evans did the equivalent of handing Chivington a loaded gun."

Chapter Three

Worshipping, Educating, Healing, Helping

own founding and city building preoccupied local leaders, but many of them also tended to religious, civic, and humanitarian affairs. Overwhelmed by rapid growth, they often played catch-up in their efforts to fashion a society worthy of being called civilized. Still, in little more than a half century, they created a city that could rightly boast of its churches, schools, orphanages, and hospitals; a community that, at least in limited ways, helped its less fortunate.

Religion

The canard that in the mid-1800s there was no God west of the Missouri River had some truth in it. Gold-rush Denver, overly supplied with rambunctious young men, certainly needed religion. Methodists full of the spirit of their founder, John Wesley, knew that and zealously embraced the task. The first church service in the Denver area was held on Sunday, November 21, 1858, a day before William H. Larimer Jr. and his party founded Denver. George W. Fisher, a Methodist lay minister and a member of Larimer's group, organized and preached at that gathering attended by about a dozen people, including two Indian women. In the summer of 1859, the Reverend Jacob Adriance, a Methodist with a fine voice, began preaching wherever he could gather a crowd. Within thirty years of the city's founding, the Methodists constructed one of the town's finest churches, Trinity United Methodist, which still stands on the northeast corner of East Eighteenth Avenue and Broadway.

Father Joseph P. Machebeuf, a French Catholic missionary, arrived in the autumn of 1860 to shepherd around two hundred people.

Joseph P. Machebeuf, who eventually became the first Roman Catholic bishop of Denver, established St. Mary's Church in 1860. Here he poses with the Sisters of Loretto and a First Communion class. Photo by Alfred E. Rinehart, courtesy Denver Public Library.

The Denver City Town Company gave him land for a church and a school. Other religious groups received similar favors because town founders knew that churches attracted families and helped ensure permanence. Machebeuf quickly built St. Mary's Church at Fifteenth and Stout Streets, tacking a little shack on the back where he slept, using a coat for a pillow and a buffalo robe for a mattress. As the city grew, so did the Roman Catholic population, until it became the largest single denomination, with dozens of parishes and schools. Its French Gothic Immaculate Conception Cathedral, dedicated in 1912, crowned Capitol Hill and gave Catholics, many of them Irish, German, and Italian immigrants, a church to rival the grand edifices raised nearby by other faiths.

The Reverend John H. Kehler, an Episcopal priest, first held services in the Criterion Saloon, where he had to compete with the ruckus raised by drinkers and gamblers. The next Sunday, Criterion customers politely kept quiet. Kehler's records indicate the challenges he faced in a town that had three dozen saloons before any churches appeared. Of his first dozen funerals, five were for gunshot victims, two for lynching victims, one for a suicide, and one for an alcoholic; only three died of natural causes. Kehler persisted and ultimately established St. John's in the Wilderness on the southeast corner of Fourteenth and Arapahoe Streets, using a building that had been abandoned by Southern Methodists, who left at the start of the Civil War. That modest structure evolved into today's stately St. John's Episcopal Cathedral at East Fourteenth Avenue and Washington Street.

Presbyterians, like other denominations, first met in saloon halls, such as the upstairs room in Apollo Hall, which also served as the town's first theater and first city hall. Churchgoers tried to concentrate on the service despite the rattling billiard balls, drunken commotion, and occasional gunfire from the bar below. When the hubbub became unbearable, the minister led his flock in a temperance hymn:

There's a spirit above and a spirit below
The spirit of love and the spirit of woe
The spirit above is the spirit divine,
The spirit below is the spirit of wine.

Not until 1862 did Presbyterians move into a $6,000 brick structure. Thirty years later they resettled into the $165,000 landmark at East Seventeenth Avenue and Sherman Street, Central Presbyterian Church, designed by the city's greatest nineteenth-century architect, Frank E. Edbrooke.

Scarcity of members kept Baptists churchless until 1866, when they started to build a holy home at Sixteenth and Curtis Streets. Lack of money forced them to stop work, leaving them with a basement, which they roofed. That dug-out church sufficed until 1873. A decade later, when there were more Baptists, they dedicated a large church between Seventeenth and Eighteenth on Stout Street. They also dispatched the Good Word throughout the state by fitting out a railroad car as a rolling chapel. In 1938 they built their stately colonial-revival landmark south of the state capitol on East Fourteenth Avenue and Grant Street.

Jewish pioneers, many of them of German or Austrian heritage, organized Temple Emanuel in 1860 and occupied their first synagogue on Curtis Street in 1875. They moved to a grand Moorish edifice at East Sixteenth Avenue and Pearl Street in 1899 and to the large contemporary-style synagogue at East First Avenue and Grape Street a half century later. Temple Emanuel's eastward migration reflected the movement of reform-minded German and Austrian Jews from their early locations in the Curtis Park neighborhood to Capitol Hill. Other Jews, many from eastern Europe with more Orthodox religious views, settled along West Colfax Avenue. Some remain there to this day, although others made a trek to the east-side Beth HaMedrosh Hagadol synagogue on Sixteenth Avenue and Gaylord Street in the 1920s. Like Temple Emanuel, it drifted farther east to an impressive synagogue and community-center complex at 560 South Monaco Parkway in the 1960s.

Many other denominations, including Christian Scientists, Congregationalists, Disciples of Christ, Lutherans, Mennonites, Mormons, Quakers, and Unitarians, planted churches in the Mile High City.

Education

First among Denver's teachers, Owen J. Goldrick arrived in the summer of 1859. The unschooled crossroads marveled at the dandily dressed pedant, who drove a wagon pulled by two oxen, which he urged on with Latin exhortations. A tall, slender man with luxuriant muttonchop sideburns and mustache, he wore soft lavender gloves, a long swallowtail coat, striped trousers, and a silk top hat. Pioneers called him "the professor." They might just as well have addressed him as "my lord," because as historian William B. Vickers recounted in his 1880 *History of Denver*, Goldrick "walked up the street with an air so lordly that people looked at him as though he had just bought the town, and would take possession as soon as the papers were made out."

Goldrick hailed from County Sligo in Ireland and supposedly studied at Trinity College in Dublin and at Columbia University in New York City. In Denver he rented a little sod-roofed log cabin along Cherry Creek, near Blake Street. There, on October 3, 1859, he opened the town's first school. He drove around in his wagon, collecting children, including Native Americans and Hispanics, charging three dollars per student per month. A couple of years later, citizens made him the town's first superintendent of schools.

Professor Owen Goldrick established Denver's first school in 1859. He rounded up students, including Hispanics and Native Americans, in his wagon, pulled by oxen he had taught to respond to his commands in Latin. Courtesy History Colorado.

Goldrick's title was grand; his educational empire was not. In 1864 the *Rocky Mountain News* listed only two public school teachers, both women. In 1865 the number dropped to one. Private schools filled part of the gap. To provide Christian education, John Evans and other Methodists opened the Colorado Seminary in 1864, a short-lived institution later resurrected as the University of Denver, originally serving children and high school–age students. Catholics opened St. Mary's Academy, staffed by the Sisters of Loretto. Episcopalians established two schools in the 1860s, Jarvis Hall for boys in Golden and Wolfe Hall in Denver for girls. Public education finally flowered with the 1873 building of the Arapahoe School between Seventeenth and Eighteenth Streets, on the north side of Arapahoe Street. This three-story "temple of learning" dominated the skyline, and its bell disturbed late risers. By admitting both blacks and whites, Arapahoe ended the segregation that marked schools in the late 1860s. In 1877 the first high school class graduated. For the rest of the century, schools in School District 1 under the high-minded stewardship of Superintendent Aaron Gove provided quality education to thousands of pupils. Children living in western and northern parts of town remained outside School District 1 until the consolidation of districts in the early twentieth century.

Among the stars of District 1 was an unusual school designed for young learners and adults, for people who wanted to learn a trade, for immigrants desperate to learn English. Thirty-six-year-old Emily Griffith, who had in her twenties served as deputy state superintendent of schools, convinced the Denver School Board in 1916 to open Opportunity School. Perhaps her way was smoothed by some other cities where progressive reformers also saw merit in helping newcomers. As Elinor Bluemel reports in her history of the school, Griffith was partly motivated by her fear that immigrants knew little about the United States, such as the one who when asked to identify Abraham Lincoln responded, "Da man that makka da pennies." She also recognized that job training could transform the lives of poor people, so she organized classes in welding, bookkeeping, and other practical endeavors. She saw special needs, so she set up a class where the deaf could learn lipreading and one for the blind to learn Braille. Criticized for training beauticians, she responded, "The day will come when there will be a beauty parlor in every little town." In 1920 Opportunity School enrolled more than 2,000 students. In 1933, the year of Griffith's retirement, the school served more than 8,000.

Between 1880 and the 1920s, the community built a school system equal to those of many older cities because its citizens were willing to pay for education, because its school officials spent the money on classroom instruction, and because they hired the city's best architects to design school buildings of charm, beauty, and civic presence. They instilled in their students and faculty an aesthetic sense and a respect for education. Today many of those splendid late-nineteenth- and early-twentieth-century schools, including East, South, West, and North High Schools, are protected as designated landmarks. By the early twentieth century, the city had also recognized an educational obligation to the general public by creating a public library crammed into a former apartment building, a history museum housed in the state capitol, and the Museum of Natural History in City Park.

From nineteenth-century beginnings, higher education also grew. Methodists kept the defunct Colorado Seminary of the 1860s alive, at least

Realizing that immigrant parents as well as children needed to learn English and job skills, Emily Griffith opened Denver's free Opportunity School in 1916, "for all who wish to learn." Courtesy Denver Public Library.

on paper, until 1880, when they poured some money into it to create the University of Denver, which by 1900 enrolled 640 students. Sacred Heart College, a Jesuit institution (later named Regis), at West Fiftieth Avenue and Lowell Boulevard, enrolled only 26 students in 1900.

Hospitals

Denver's hospitals in the 1860s were, like its schools, small and short-lived. Fifteen years passed between the town's establishment and Dr. John Elsner's 1873 founding of a public hospital, which also served as a poorhouse for the indigent until the mid-1880s. Then the down-and-out were shunted off to the Arapahoe County Poor Farm in Globeville, a few miles north of town, where they grew vegetables and breathed fumes from nearby smelters. Rather than rely on the limited compassion of the city, many Denverites sought help from private hospitals, such as St. Joseph's (1873) and St. Anthony's (1892), both Roman Catholic institutions staffed by nuns; St. Luke's (1881), affiliated with the Episcopal Church; Children's (1908); Presbyterian (1926); and Porter Memorial (1930).

For more than a half century, the city was itself a big hospital. Hundreds of thousands of people suffered from tuberculosis (TB) in the

United States. The insidious lung disease sometimes abated if victims rested and got plenty of sunshine and fresh air. Denver had both and as a result attracted health seekers, just as it had once enticed gold seekers. The blessing was mixed. Some TB victims lived on accumulated capital or were supported by friends and relatives. Others with scant means desperately gambled their meager savings to come to Denver, where they often died alone and penniless. The city did not want them—lawmakers considered making them wear warning bells—and did practically nothing to help them.

National organizations were more generous. When the depression of 1893 sank Frances Wisebart Jacobs's plans for a TB hospital for Jews, B'nai B'rith, a national Jewish philanthropic organization, raised the money to open it in 1899. The National Jewish Hospital for Consumptives admitted both Jews and non-Jews and treated both for free. The Jewish Consumptives' Relief Society, (JCRS) under the direction of Dr. Charles Spivak, begged funds from near and far to create the JCRS hospital west of Denver, near

The Jewish Consumptives' Relief Society on West Colfax Avenue took in Jews and Gentiles, even dying patients, and charged no one for admission and treatment for tuberculosis, the country's number-one killer. Courtesy Tom Noel Collection.

West Colfax and Pierce Streets, in 1904. Like National Jewish, JCRS provided free care, but unlike National Jewish, it followed kosher dietary rules and hence attracted Orthodox Jews. Swedish groups from across the country helped fund the Swedish National Sanatorium, south of Denver in Englewood. Immigrants from the Netherlands represented by the Christian Reformed Church and the Reformed Church in America made Bethesda in southern Denver possible. German Lutherans sponsored the Evangelical Lutheran Sanatorium, a tent colony at its inception in 1905, to the west of Denver in Wheat Ridge. Millionaire Lawrence C. Phipps built the Agnes Phipps Memorial Sanatorium (1904) in eastern Denver to honor his mother. The largest TB facility, Fitzsimons, federally funded as an army hospital, took root east of Denver in Aurora after World War I.

Charities

Men often got the credit for establishing churches, schools, libraries, hospitals, and charities, but much of the actual work was done by female teachers, librarians, and nurses. One of the first to take compassionate action was Elizabeth "Libby" Byers, who in the summer of 1859 joined her husband, William, editor of the *Rocky Mountain News*, in Denver, where she moved into a rude sod house. Reflecting on the deaths of two of her four children, she reminisced years later: "Had I known of the hardships and experiences which lay before me in this pioneer country all the gold in the mountains could not have induced me to come."

While William touted Denver as the city of opportunity, Elizabeth worried about those without opportunity. In January 1860, she helped organize the first known charitable institution in Denver, the Ladies' Union Aid Society, which was also the town's first women's organization. She presided over the meetings and collected the ten-cent monthly dues. The society made underwear, nightshirts, and bandages for the Colorado Civil War soldiers and helped the poor.

Elizabeth got sisterly support from Margaret Gray Evans, wife of Governor John Evans. They worked with Ella Vincent, another prominent Methodist, to host a social for all the "old ladies" they could find. Discovering widows and other elderly women living in loneliness and poverty, they reorganized the Ladies' Union Aid Society as the Ladies' Relief Society in 1874 and built the Old Ladies' Home. Renamed the

Argyle, it remains a refuge for seniors at 4115 West Thirty-Eighth Avenue. The Ladies' Relief Society also opened an Industrial Home for Working Girls and ran a wood yard, where men and boys exchanged their labor for food and shelter. By the 1880s, the society operated a day nursery, a free kindergarten, a free medical dispensary, and depots for distributing clothing and supplies and made hundreds of home visits each year. The largest single charity in Colorado, the Ladies' Relief Society by 1889 annually raised and spent some ten thousand dollars to assist 2,610 persons. Protestants, Catholics, and Jews all sat on its advisory board.

Elizabeth Byers encouraged Margaret Evans to establish the Denver Orphans' Home in 1872. Supported by many women, including Elizabeth Iliff, wife of cattle baron John Iliff, and Eliza Routt, wife of Governor John Routt, this home for poor, neglected, and homeless children thrives to this day as the Denver Children's Home. The Young Women's Christian Association also owes thanks to Margaret Evans and other women for its first local chapter, established in 1887. Seeing an additional need, Elizabeth Byers in 1887 set up the Working Boys' Home and School, hoping to keep poor boys out of trouble with "as pure and homelike an influence as can be obtained in any institutional atmosphere." In 1902 this refuge was renamed the Elizabeth M. Byers Home for Boys.

It was one of the few tributes Elizabeth collected. In 1899 she declined the honor of a stained-glass window in the Colorado state capitol, saying her family was already represented there by her husband and that other women were equally deserving. A typescript of an interview with her preserved in the Denver Public Library's Western History Department reveals her thinking: "While I gladly accord my husband every honor he is entitled to, and rejoice that he is so honored and appreciated by his fellow-citizens, I remember that he and I stood shoulder to shoulder through all the trials and hardships of pioneer life, and I feel that I ought not stand wholly in the light of reflected glory."

The honor of a capitol dome window went instead to Frances Wisebart Jacobs, a coworker with Elizabeth Byers in the Ladies' Relief Society and a leader in the Hebrew Ladies' Benevolent Society. From the time she arrived in 1874 to her death in 1892, she labored to provide medicine for TB sufferers, to aid homeless women, and to bring food and soap to the poor. With others in 1887, she formed an umbrella group, the Charity

Organization Society, that foreshadowed today's United Way. In the early 1890s, she helped raise the money that eventually led to the establishment of the National Jewish Hospital for Consumptives, which survives as National Jewish Health, one of the nation's finest respiratory hospitals. There a small statue memorializes Jacobs, and she is included in the National Women's Hall of Fame in Seneca, New York.

In 1996, two years after inducting Jacobs, the National Women's Hall of Fame recognized the work of Mother Frances Xavier Cabrini, another woman with a Colorado connection. This Italian nun and her Missionary Sisters of the Sacred Heart founded numerous orphanages in the United States and other countries. In Denver she established the Queen of Heaven Orphanage at Forty-Ninth Avenue and Federal Boulevard, site today of a motel. Other orphanages, such as the Mount Saint Vincent Orphan Asylum (1882), a large Catholic institution at West Forty-Second Avenue and Lowell Boulevard, and Clayton College, in northeastern Denver at Colorado and Martin Luther King Jr. Boulevards, over the years cared for thousands of children whose parents were either dead or unable to support them. Both, though no longer orphanages, maintain their mission to serve children. In 1946 Pope Pius XII canonized Mother Cabrini, the first US citizen to be so honored. Her shrine atop a hill near Interstate 70 a few miles west of the city remains a popular place for pilgrims.

In the Colorado Capitol a window dedicated in 1977 honors another saintly philanthropist, "Aunt" Clara Brown. A freed slave, she took part in the 1859 gold rush, working as a wagon-train cook. She prospered as a laundress in Central City, where she supported many good causes, including St. James Methodist Church. She also helped many of her relatives move to Colorado. Dying in Denver in 1885, she was honored by state and city officials and buried at Riverside Cemetery by the Society of Colorado Pioneers. Like John H. Kehler, Elizabeth Byers, Margaret Gray Evans, Aaron Gove, and many others, Clara Brown made Denver and Colorado more civilized and decent places.

Chapter Four

Growing Out and Up

*D*enver's population exploded in the thirty years between 1870, when it had fewer than 5,000 people, and 1900, when it counted more than 130,000. Maps changed yearly, suburbs sprouted and were often gobbled up by Denver, and business directories got fatter, as did the portfolios of home builders, real estate speculators, utility magnates, and transit moguls as Colorado's chief city built out and up.

Geography, Topography, and Grids

Mother Nature gave the city plenty of easily accessible land. Low hills rarely proved troublesome to carriages or streetcars. Cherry Creek could be easily crossed via short bridges. The South Platte River offered more of a barrier and coupled, with the railroad tracks that mainly ran along its eastern bank, retarded westward growth, but it too was bridged and eventually viaducts allowed traffic to flow above the rail yards. The land was well suited to a grid layout of streets and avenues common in many American cities. Pioneers initially thought in terms of grids and laid out streets that paralleled Cherry Creek and the South Platte River, neither of which ran along straight north–south and east–west lines. Hence, the town developed in the 1860s on an angular grid. Late in the 1860s when Henry C. Brown platted his land on Brown's Bluff, a barren parcel of land east by a mile of the central business district, he sensibly laid out his Capitol Hill subdivision with streets that ran north and south and avenues that ran east and west. Where his grid collided with the earlier grid, surveyors and streets went crazy, and odd-shaped triangles of land resulted. On one of them, Brown built the triangular-shaped Brown Palace Hotel, at Seventeenth Street and Broadway, in 1892.

Streetcars

Other developers generally followed Brown's example, giving much of the city a grid layout that made most addresses easy to find and facilitated transportation. Beginning in the 1870s and lasting until they were gradually supplanted by automobiles in the twentieth century, streetcar lines allowed rapid expansion in all directions. The first streetcar line, the Denver Horse Railroad Company, used horses to pull cars along railroad tracks installed in city streets. That line originated in 1871 in the town's oldest neighborhood, Auraria, and ran up Larimer Street to Sixteenth Street, down Sixteenth to Champa Street, and then shot out Champa to the end of the line at Twenty-Seventh Street. There, out in open prairie, people built homes in the city's first streetcar suburb, Curtis Park.

Sometimes the company used mules rather than horses to pull its coaches, so it rebranded itself as the Denver City Railway Company because the word *mule* did not lend itself to corporate titles. It built its second line in 1873, starting at Fifteenth and Larimer and running northwest on Fifteenth across the railroad tracks

Passengers disembarking at Union Station could walk across Wynkoop Street to the Denver City Railway Company for a horse-drawn streetcar ride to the city's proliferating suburbs. Courtesy Denver Public Library.

and over the South Platte River to the then largely vacant Highlands. Its third line extended the Sixteenth Street tracks to Broadway and then south on Broadway to Cherry Creek, fostering growth in Capitol Hill, the city's most elegant residential district. The Park Avenue line, also established in 1874, took a diagonal route along Twenty-Third Street from Champa to Park Avenue, spurring development in the neighborhoods of Five Points, North Capitol Hill, and City Park. By 1884 the Denver City Railway tallied fifteen and a half miles of track, forty-five cars, two hundred horses, one hundred employees, and a headquarters and car barn on Seventeenth Street, opposite Union Station. Commercial and residential real estate flourished along the tracks, particularly on Sixteenth Street, which became the city's major retail strip. In 1889 a rival company, the Denver City Cable Railway Company, began installing underground cables similar to those in San Francisco. The offices, power plant, and car barns opened in an elegant brick two-story building still standing at Eighteenth and Lawrence Streets. By the early 1890s, city promoters boasted of one of the country's more extensive cable-car networks.

The Denver Tramway Company (DTC) emerged as the giant among at least a dozen local transit firms and by 1900 had driven practically all of the others out of business. Its prime mover, John Evans, brought the Denver Pacific Railway to the city in 1870. In 1886 he and others incorporated the Denver Tramway Company to build electric lines. The company installed a citywide network of overhead electric trolleys for lines that reached practically every neighborhood. In fact, the DTC created neighborhoods by running tracks into undeveloped areas, such as University Park, more than three miles southeast of downtown. The DTC shot out East Colfax Avenue to Park Hill, Montclair, and Aurora and out West Colfax and West Thirteenth Avenue to Lakewood and Golden. One of the busiest lines went south on Broadway to Englewood and Littleton. Another headed west on Thirty-Second Avenue to Wheat Ridge and Arvada, and yet another served Globeville and Adams County.

The DTC became one of the city's biggest employers and an essential part of most people's lives. Neighborhood shops clustered where its lines intersected, and home builders developed land within walking distance of the streetcar routes. Few people could afford to maintain a horse and buggy; most either lived near where they worked or took streetcars to work, shop, and play. Special tramway cars were rented for weddings and honeymoons. Funeral cars A and B took many people on their final rides—to Riverside and Fairmount Cemeteries.

Neighborhoods

Creation of the streetcar suburbs was hastened by the transformation of pioneer neighborhoods. Auraria, after the railroads arrived, evolved into an industrial area pungent with the aromas of breweries, bakeries, and flour mills. Many Aurarians moved out, giving way to poorer people seeking cheap housing near factory jobs. North of Cherry Creek, the rapidly expanding central business district overran residential blocks. As commercial buildings leapfrogged uptown, homes, even many of the great houses along Fourteenth Street, were converted to boardinghouses and stores. Streetcar lines were laid to the north to industrial suburbs named for the smelters they served—Argo, Swansea, and Globeville. Immigrants crowded these districts, finding work in the fiery ore furnaces. Within the shadows of smelter smokestacks, blue-collar families rented —or built their own—cheap shanties.

More affluent, status-sensitive people sought homes east and south of downtown. In the 1870s and 1880s, some were impressed with the area around Curtis Park, the city's first public park. Families with money took streetcars out Larimer, Curtis, Champa, Stout, and Welton Streets to look at brick homes dressed in the fashionable Italianate style, with flat roofs, high-ceilinged rooms, elongated windows, brick corbeling, and elegantly framed front porches. Real estate agents pointed out that Mayor Wolfe Londoner, dry goods merchant J. Jay Joslin, and former territorial governor William Gilpin had all moved to Curtis Park.

Streetcar lines also spread the middle- and upper-middle classes into the City Park, Park Hill, Harman (now Cherry Creek North), and Montclair neighborhoods. In these fashionable east-side suburbs, promoters offered 50-by-125-foot lots rather than the standard 25-by-125-foot lots. Spacious yards pleased suburbanites; flower gardens, lawns, and vegetable patches enabled the bourgeoisie to raise their children amid bumblebees and greenery, away from the saloons, blacksmith shops, and boardinghouses that characterized older parts of the city. Aping the late-nineteenth-century architectural tastes of people in Chicago,

St. Louis, and other midwestern and eastern cities, Denverites also replicated the greenery of the wetter places from which most of them had come. They planted trees and lawns that they watered from ditches, wells, and eventually underground water mains and pipes. That all of this ignored the reality of the area's hot summers and semiarid climate did not overly concern them.

Southeast of the central business district, Henry C. Brown developed his land on what was originally called Brown's Bluff as a wealthy residential neighborhood known as Capitol Hill. By the late 1880s, it was far more fashionable than Fourteenth Street, where many of the city's early nabobs, such as John Evans and Nathaniel Hill, lived. As Capitol Hill filled up, other wealthy people located a mile or so to the southeast, near Mount Prospect, the cemetery established by William Larimer Jr. in 1861. The cemetery, which the town had purchased in 1872, presented a problem. By the late 1880s, it had become a weed-infested derelict necropolis, a hindrance to upscale development in the area. On March 16, 1887, the *Denver Republican* newspaper observed, "It is so ugly, that if there are any buried there with any sense of the artistic, or longings for the beautiful, they might turn over in their graves and groan at the thought of what is above them."

In the early 1890s, the city decided to enliven the neighborhood by turning the bleak boneyard into a park. Its ten thousand silent residents were slated to sleep in newer, larger, better-kept cemeteries—Riverside (1876), Fairmount (1890), and Mount Olivet (1890). Undertaker Edward P. McGovern was offered $1.90 for each box of remains he dug up. Unearthing an opportunity to quadruple his money, he subdivided corpses into as many as four boxes. Appalled onlookers reported McGovern's macabre misdeeds, and he was dismissed, leaving graves and bones in a disheveled landscape looking like a poorly planned resurrection on the last day. One grave was left with the casket lid shattered, a partly decomposed gentleman staring out for two weeks. Finally, the city plowed under corpses and graves. The cemetery became Congress Park and then Cheesman Park, named in honor of water company president and real estate tycoon Walter Cheesman, who died in 1907. His widow donated the park's elegant Colorado Yule marble Cheesman Pavilion, with its splendid view of the Front Range of the Rockies. Overlooking the park's past, millionaires, including *Denver Post* publishers Frederick G. Bonfils and Harry H. Tammen, built mansions nearby. Beneath Cheesman's rolling lawns and the Botanic Garden's prized plants, an estimated two thousand remains still lay unclaimed and forgotten.

Parks often spur development. City Park, a couple of miles east of Cheesman, led to the creation of Park Hill, touted as a haven for the well-to-do. Located on high ground east of the park, it was platted in 1887 by an eccentric German, Baron Eugene A. von Winkler. This character came to Denver after being sacked from the Prussian army, reportedly for falling off his horse in the presence of the kaiser. He purchased a large tract east of Colorado Boulevard, announcing that he would build a racetrack surrounded by a posh residential subdivision. His exotic plans for a racecourse did not survive his suicide, but saner developers, including park commissioner Warwick Downing, picked up the pieces of Baron von Winkler's dream and platted the finest of Park Hill's subdivisions, Downington.

Southeast of Park Hill lay Montclair, platted by another German baron, Walter von Richthofen, shortly before his friend Baron von Winkler laid out Park Hill. Richthofen, uncle of Manfred von Richthofen, the "Red Baron" of World War I aviation fame, had come to Denver in the 1870s. In 1885 he announced the grand opening of Montclair, "The Beautiful Suburban Town of Denver." At East Twelfth Avenue and Olive Street, Richthofen erected his own still-standing castle as a show home. Strict ordinances guarded Montclair. One regulation forbade the use of "common, vulgar, indecent, abusive or improper language." Despite the lure of the castle, the moral atmosphere, and Montclair's trolley connections via East Colfax and East Eighth Avenues, the baron found it difficult to attract buyers.

A similar fate befell Edwin and Louise Harman, who platted their 320-acre farm on the north bank of Cherry Creek, between University and Colorado Boulevards, as the town site of Harman. Harman boasted a streetcar line, a still-standing town hall at East Fourth Avenue and St. Paul Street, a stone schoolhouse, and seventy-five-dollar lots. Reflecting the haphazard, spotty development of the suburban fringe, neither Montclair nor Harman fully blossomed until the coming of the automobile and the post–World War II boom.

Like other suburban developers, Baron Walter von Richthofen promoted his town Montclair as a healthy escape from the crowded, congested, crime-filled city. Note the streetcar in the foreground next to St. Luke's Episcopal Church, a surviving Montclair landmark, as is the baron's castle and show home at East Twelfth Avenue and Olive Street. Courtesy Tom Noel Collection.

South Denver, stretching from Alameda to Yale Avenues and from Colorado Boulevard on the east to the South Platte River on the west, embraced nearly twelve square miles, making it Denver's largest suburb. In 1890 most of its 1,491 residents lived close to transit lines extending from the central business district. Promoter James A. Fleming donated his home, which still stands at 1510 South Grant Street, as a town hall while serving as mayor. His brothers opened a lumberyard and built blocks of homes at a time. "It seems no more trouble for them to build a house," noted South Denver's newspaper, the *Denver Eye*, "than it is for a shoemaker to make a pair of shoes." Concern about the saloons, dance halls, and gambling joints clustered around Overland Park racetrack led South Denverites to incorporate in 1886 in order to crack down on vice. After the town imposed an annual saloon license fee of thirty-five hundred dollars, the *Denver Eye* observed that "roadhouses and saloons were all cleaned out."

Baker, on the west side of Broadway between West Sixth and West Ellsworth Avenues, and University Park, home of the University of Denver after 1890, were among many communities that never became incorporated towns. The Broadway streetcar reached Orchard Place

(Englewood), which did incorporate. Beyond lay the country town of Littleton, which grew up around Richard Little's Rough and Ready Flour Mill in the 1860s. Englewood and Littleton, together with Aurora, Golden, and Lakewood, formed an outer ring of suburbs tied to Denver by streetcars.

Regis University in northwestern Denver has grown, with branch campuses. It is still owned and operated by the Jesuits, an order of Catholic priests noted for their scholarship. Photo by Tom Noel.

Areas east of the South Platte River were initially more accessible to the city center, but viaducts and bridges gradually opened up southwest and northwest sections. By 1888 the southwest suburbs of Valverde and Barnum claimed a few residents who saw their neighborhoods grow slowly, despite the promotion of circus king Phineas T. Barnum, who claimed the area had the finest climate in the world. North of Barnum, Villa Park with its twisting lanes gave people a chance to escape from the monotonous street grid that dominated most of the city.

Northwest Denver grew rapidly after streetcar lines crossed the railroad tracks and the river via Fifteenth and Sixteenth Street viaducts. Temperance advocate Horatio B. Pearce had platted the town of Highlands on his ranch in 1871. After getting himself elected mayor, Pearce inexplicably moved to saloon-saturated Denver. His town, however, persevered, growing to more than five thousand residents in 1890, when it ranked as Colorado's sixth-largest city. Besides seven transit lines, there were other "secrets of Highlands' success" according to the town's report for 1891: "True to her name and nature, she stands high and sightly, where the pure air from the mountains—that God-given slayer of disease—is used firsthand by her people and swells their lungs with strength and healthfulness." Northwest of Highlands, John Brisben Walker and Scottish capitalist Dr. William Bell grew alfalfa at Berkeley Farm until the late 1880s. Then they turned their $1,000 investment into $325,000 by selling the acreage to a Kansas City syndicate that developed the town of Berkeley. With a lake, a large park, and a small Jesuit college (Regis), Berkeley had much to offer. Like Highlands, it puffed its pure air and pure morals.

The suburban ring included both unincorporated "additions" to the city and a dozen incorporated towns with their own officials and services. Many of these towns became financially strapped during the 1893 depression and accepted annexation to Denver as a fiscal solution. Such was the case with Barnum, Harman, Highlands, and South Denver. Creation of the City and County of Denver in 1902 brought into the city limits the towns of Berkeley, Elyria, Globeville, Montclair, and Valverde.

Growing Up

Street railroads radiated from Denver's core, making the business district easily accessible to shoppers and workers and concentrating most commercial activity in the city's center. In the 1880s, the cost of downtown land shot up, prompting developers to squeeze value from their lots by building multistory buildings. In the early 1880s, large edifices such as the Tabor Grand Opera House made most pre-1880 structures look puny, and in the late 1880s and early 1890s, Denver built buildings that, borrowing a term from high-flying baseballs, they called skyscrapers. Among them were the Mining Exchange Building at Fifteenth and Arapahoe Streets, the Boston Building at Seventeenth and Champa Streets, and the Equitable Building at Seventeenth and Stout Streets. Most elegant of all, the nine-story Brown Palace Hotel demonstrated the architectural genius of Frank E. Edbrooke, whose inspired use of a triangular piece of land well served Henry C. Brown, the hotel's owner. The Brown Palace introduced visitors to the wonders of the age—steel frame construction and indoor plumbing, elevators, and electricity. A city

within a city, it had its own power plant, bakery, two artesian wells, and various shops and services. A hotel publication boasted that the Brown could handle all of a guest's needs, from birth (with assistance of the house physician) to death. The Corliss engine in the basement that supplied both heat and power was said to burn hot enough to be used as a crematorium, should the need arise.

The Brown Palace Hotel, Denver's finest hotel ever since its 1892 opening, remains a favorite palace of the public, where celebrity spotters have seen nearly every US president since Theodore Roosevelt. Courtesy Denver Public Library.

With a population of more than one hundred thousand, a grand hotel, elegant neighborhoods, handsome schools, and churches, Denver had become a proud city by the end of its 1870–92 boom. From 1892 to 1900, it was to suffer a serious downturn, but then the economy improved. Smelters, flour mills, brewers, and even a rubber factory were all to contribute to the city's prosperity.

Chapter Five

Go-Getters and Gamblers

*D*enver's boom between 1870 and 1892 ended with the silver crash of 1893 but resumed again after 1900, bringing the population to 256,491 in 1920. Without strong economic foundations, that growth would have been impossible. Smelters, railroad shops, slaughterhouses, flour mills, mining machinery, and other manufacturers collectively employed thousands. The city's attorneys drew clients from throughout the state; its hotels lodged visitors from faraway places; its theaters and amusement parks entertained residents and tourists. Saloons, gambling dens, and brothels capitalized on vice.

Smelters

Placer miners could recover gold dust from river sands by amalgamating it with mercury, a dangerous but fairly simple process. Lode miners who followed veins of gold deep into the earth were not so lucky, because it was exceedingly difficult to unlock pure gold from the ore with which it was chemically bound. Perplexed mine owners persuaded Nathaniel P. Hill, a chemistry professor from Brown University in Rhode Island, to come to Colorado in 1864 to study the complex ores. Backed by Boston capital, he organized the Boston and Colorado Smelting Company in 1867. Within a few years, aided by Richard Pearce, a world-class metallurgist from Cornwall, England, Boston and Colorado's smelter in Black Hawk was refining ores. In 1878 the operation moved to Argo, a new suburb along the South Platte a few miles north of Denver. Other smelters, including the Omaha and Grant and the Globe, located nearby, creating an impressive industrial complex dominated by massive smelter chimneys far taller than any downtown building.

Hill built a mansion on Fourteenth Street and in 1879 entered politics at the top by snatching a US Senate seat, a prize sought by many a tycoon. Securing that honor was easier then because state legislators selected US senators, and those legislators often favored rich men who gave them generous campaign contributions. When the *Rocky Mountain News* attacked Hill as a fat cat who bought his office, he tried to silence the *News* by buying it. Its editor sneered that Hill could subscribe "at ten dollars a year, which is just as near as Mr. Hill will ever come to owning it." So he established his own newspaper, the *Denver Republican*, which became a major competitor for the *News* and remained an important paper from its 1879 birth until its 1913 demise. Predictably, it represented the interests of the Republican Party, of business, and of Nathaniel P. Hill.

By the early twentieth century, another smelter operator, John Simon Guggenheim (usually known by his middle name), had emerged as one of the city's most powerful men because his family controlled the giant American Smelting and Refining Company (ASARCO), which by 1901 had acquired most of the local smelters. Like Hill, Guggenheim wanted to be a

The Argo Smelter, now buried under the intersection of I-25 and I-70, opened in 1879, the first of the city's giant smelters. Courtesy Tom Noel Collection.

US senator, so he used his money to get the job, which he held from 1907 to 1913. Labor leaders condemned him for the working conditions at his smelters. Progressive reformers lambasted him for buying his office, and environmentalists now decry the pollution that ASARCO left behind. Buildings he donated to the Colorado School of Mines, Colorado State University, the University of Northern Colorado, and the University of Colorado also make up part of his legacy. After leaving Colorado in 1912, his fortune grew even greater, allowing him and his foundation to fund hundreds of millions of dollars in Guggenheim Fellowships, named for Simon's son John, who died at age seventeen in 1922.

Hill, Guggenheim, and others won the gamble on gold and silver. In subsequent years, the city prospered not only from precious metals but also from Colorado and its neighboring states' prodigious stores of molybdenum, lead, zinc, uranium, vanadium, tungsten, copper, coal, oil, natural gas, and other buried resources. To this day, booms and busts in fossil-fuel production create Denver's ups and downs.

Processing

Just as the city benefited from statewide mining activity, it reaped riches from farms and ranches. In 1870 Colorado tallied fewer than eighteen hundred farms; by 1920 the number approached sixty thousand. Much of the state's wheat flowed to Denver to be milled by Colorado Milling and Elevator. Brewers such as Denver's Tivoli-Union and Golden's Coors turned barley and hops into beer. Ranchers sent their cattle to the city's stockyards to be fed and slaughtered. Bulky sugar beets were usually processed in towns near where they were grown, but Denver shared the wealth as the headquarters for the Great Western Sugar Company, whose office building (now repurposed) is a National Register Historic Landmark on the southeast corner of Wazee Street and the Sixteenth Street Mall.

Adolph Coors Sr., Charles Boettcher, and John Kernan Mullen, whose names were to loom large in local history, owed their prominence to their commonsense realization that they could make money doing mundane things. Prussian-born Adolph Coors arrived in Denver in 1873 and soon set up a brewery in nearby Golden, on the banks of

Adolph Coors, a German immigrant orphan, created Colorado's best-known brand. Coors used technological advances such as steam-powered machinery, the crown cap instead of corks, and refrigerated railcars to ship his beer to ever-broadening markets. Courtesy Denver Public Library.

Clear Creek. Prohibition, which began in Colorado on New Year's Day 1916, earlier than in much of the rest of the nation, forced Coors to diversify into making malted milk, near beer, pottery, and porcelain. Sadly, Adolph, who leaped to his death on June 5, 1929, did not see the day in 1933 when Coors could again sell beer. Other local brewers competed with Coors, but in the end the Golden brewery, controlled for more than a century by the Coors family, became one of the nation's major brewers, before it merged with Molson in 2005 and then worked out a marketing alliance with SABMiller to form an international fermenting colossus.

Charles Boettcher was also born in Prussia (today part of Germany). Arriving in the United States at age seventeen in 1869, he sold hardware in Cheyenne, Greeley, Fort Collins, and Boulder before taking a calculated risk on boomtown Leadville in 1879. In little more than a decade, his hardware business and banking endeavors made him rich enough to escape from the Cloud City. In the early 1890s, he settled in Denver, where with immense energy he pursued numerous ventures, including sugar beet processing, cement making, mining, meatpacking, ranching, banking, railroads, real estate, life insurance, and manufacturing blasting powder. Eventually, Charles, who enjoyed relaxing at his Lorraine Lodge on Lookout Mountain, let his son, Claude, command the family's enterprises, but Charles remained active in business until a few years before his death in 1948 at age ninety-six. Claude, a behind-the-scenes power in local and state politics, died at eighty-two in 1957, and without his guidance much of his empire faded. The Boettcher Foundation kept the family name alive by funding scholarships and supporting culture. In the late 1950s, it made one of its most heralded gifts, Claude's home at East Eighth Avenue and Logan Street, which became the official residence of Colorado's governors.

Like Coors and Boettcher, John Kernan Mullen, known by his initials, J. K., was a naturalized US citizen, having been born in Ireland in 1847. Poverty forced his family to emigrate in the mid-1850s to Oriskany Falls, New York, where John learned the flour-milling business. He brought that skill with him in 1871 to Denver, where at first he toiled digging a ditch to supply water to a flour mill. Hard work, luck, and risk taking—he borrowed heavily to finance his operations—paid off. In *Pride of the Rockies: The Life of Colorado's Premier Irish Patron, John Kernan Mullen,* historian Bill Convery Jr. writes: "Combined J. K. Mullen and Co. and its competitors made Denver the leading mill city in the West. . . . In 1883 [Denver mills] produced an estimated 432,000 sacks of flour worth $975,000, as well as bran, cornmeal, and feed worth $329,500. J. K. Mullen and Co. manufactured almost half of the total."

When area millers formed the Colorado Milling and Elevator Company in 1885, Mullen became its president. Millions upon millions of sacks of flour made him millions upon millions of dollars. Among the most generous of the city's rich, he aided numerous causes, many connected to the Roman Catholic Church. He helped build the Cathedral of the Immaculate Conception and Saint Cajetan's Church at Ninth and Lawrence Streets. His wife, Catherine, prompted him to support Saint Joseph Hospital and the Mount Saint Vincent Orphanage, both founded by the Sisters of Charity of Leavenworth. His compassion toward old people led him to establish the J. K. Mullen Home for the Aged in 1917 on acreage near West Thirtieth Avenue and Lowell Boulevard. He was planning his best-known benefaction—Mullen Home for Boys, which

evolved into Mullen High School at 3601 South Lowell Boulevard—
when he died on August 9, 1929.

Manufacturing

Denver's remoteness from heavily populated parts of the country made
it difficult to establish large manufacturing establishments in the city because shipping goods long distances added to their cost. Moreover, railroads controlled by eastern moguls, who sometimes had manufacturing
investments in other cities, could strangle Denver industry by charging
high freight rates. The city's early-twentieth-century hopes of becoming an automobile manufacturing hub faded, as did its dreams of milling cotton. George J. Kindle, a mattress maker, got so angry about high
freight rates that he ran for the US House of Representatives, but even
his election in 1912 could not get Denver fair treatment.

Entrepreneurial skill and good luck could, however, sometimes
overcome transportation barriers, as Charles Gates and his brother
John demonstrated. Initially, their Gates Rubber Company (founded in
1911 under a different name) made covers designed to extend tire wear.
Later, thanks to John's invention of the V-Belt and Charles's business
genius, it became a major manufacturer of hoses and belts. For much
of the twentieth century, Denverites proudly showed their out-of-town
cousins Gates's twenty-five-square-block factory complex (now demolished), stretching south of Mississippi Avenue along South Broadway, to
prove that Denver had big industry. Charles Sr. died in 1961. His son,
Charles Jr., sold the rubber company in 1996 for more than a billion dollars. Across Broadway from Gates, the Shwayder brothers manufactured
Samsonite luggage, which, like Gates's V-Belts, found a national market
and gave locals yet another reason to brag.

Gamblers Galore

The Gateses and the Shwayders took risks in tune with the city's past, for
it was founded by gamblers. Some bet they could strike golden riches;
some hoped to reap real estate rewards. Others saw gambling itself as a
way to mint money. "Poker" Alice Tubbs, Edward Chase, Vaso Chucovich,
John Henry "Doc" Holliday, Bat Masterson, Jefferson Randolph "Soapy"

Smith, and other noted gamblers operated in Denver in the late 1800s. Soapy Smith, the slipperiest of the knights of the green cloth, had flimflammed Leadville before unpacking his carpetbag on Denver's Larimer Street in 1883. He began selling soap. Not just ordinary soap, he assured curious onlookers. They watched as he inserted fifty-dollar bills between the soap and its wrapper and began a pitch that went something like this: "Step right up, pards, and flirt with lady luck. You can't lose with soap. Cleanliness is next to godliness. When you raise your arm, do you lose your charm? And the feel of these crisp new greenbacks is heavenliness. This soap is made in my own factory with my special formula. It will cure baldness and wash away the gray. Enhance your manhood; mesmerize the ladies. Wash away your troubles; wash away your sins today."

Only Soapy's shills recovered the soap with the big bills, although many offered to buy at one dollar a bar and get the chance to pick out the bonanza bars. Few ended up with anything more than a nickel cake of ordinary soap. When police arrested him, he balked at giving his full name, so they booked him as "Soapy Smith." In court Soapy offered to convince the judge of his innocence by demonstrating his soap game. He carefully wrapped the soap in tissue paper and, after catching the judge's eye, inserted a one-hundred-dollar bill. At an appropriate moment, the judge pocketed the bill and found Soapy innocent. Or so goes one of the many legends about this slippery character. Soapy convinced the police that his soap sales could also be profitable for them. They allowed him to operate as long as he did not con residents, only out-of-towners.

Soapy also enjoyed politics. He ingratiated himself with the Republican gang, many of them connected with brewers and saloonkeepers, who ran city hall. He became a star voter recruiter and a poll watcher. Bums, tramps, and underworld dregs got to vote, early and often. In the 1889 mayoral election, voters were rewarded with free drinks and cash as they rushed around town to vote in multiple precincts. Wolfe Londoner, the victor in that contest, collected so many fraudulent votes that the Colorado Supreme Court ordered him to vacate his office in 1891. Always in search of fresh suckers to fleece, Soapy wound up in Skagway, Alaska, where vigilantes gunned him down on July 8, 1898, and laid him in his grave.

Gamblers such as Soapy often either went into the saloon business

Mattie Silks, the most successful of Denver's madams, operated three Market Street bordellos, one of which has been restored at 1942 Market Street. Courtesy History Colorado.

or allied themselves with saloon owners, pimps, prostitutes, and the madams who gave Denver a reputation as a wide-open town, until reformers spruced up the city's image after 1912. For many years, amateur historians portrayed the sordid sex trade as harmless frontier fun. In recent decades, realization that economic hardship drove some girls as young as ten into prostitution, that sexually transmitted syphilis ate away people's brains and eventually killed, as did botched abortions, and that some women saw suicide as the only escape has caused scholars to see the trade as the nightmare it was.

Family Entertainment

Proud of being the state's political and business hub, Denver suffered from its reputation as a sinful place—masking its offense by confining its vice district to older parts of downtown along Market and Larimer Streets. It could also rightly claim that it offered citizens and visitors wholesome diversions. They could, for example, watch a play at the Tabor Grand Opera House or another of downtown's theaters, many of them along Curtis Street, which, illuminated at night, became a great

Silver-mining king Horace Tabor poured part of his fortune into the Tabor Grand Opera House at Sixteenth and Curtis Streets. Its magnificent curtain bore words prophetic for the theater, demolished in 1964: "So fleet the Works of Man, Back to the earth again. Ancient and holy things fade like a dream." Courtesy History Colorado.

white way. As movies crowded out stage shows and vaudeville acts, many of the theaters turned into movie houses, where people could see one of their town's best-known sons, Douglas Fairbanks Sr., born Douglas Ullman in Denver in 1883, star in such silent films as *Robin Hood* and *The Mask of Zorro*. There too they could watch another silent-film star, one-time Denverite Maude Fealy, whose beauty and talent made her a stage and screen star.

In North Denver three amusement parks offered people recreation beyond the commonplace. Manhattan Beach, established in 1891 on the shore of Sloan's Lake, fizzled and is barely remembered today. Elitch's and Lakeside have survived for more than a century. John and Mary Elitch opened Elitch's Gardens in 1890 on rural land at Thirty-Eighth Avenue and Tennyson Street. Mary so loved the trees and gardens that after John's death in 1891, she continued to manage the park on her own. It took a lot of management because it was an extraordinary place, combining rides, a ballroom, a theater, and a zoo that featured pajama-clad monkeys, seals, bears, and a white buffalo that mingled with the park guests. A small-scale railroad train took guests for short rides, while Mary rode in a cart pulled by an ostrich. At Elitch's Denverites saw their first motion picture on August 14, 1896, but its stage plays over the years drew the most attention. Operating in the summer for a century, the theater attracted top talent—from Sarah Bernhardt to Grace Kelly to Mickey Rooney.

When Mary fell on hard times in 1915, J. K. Mullen saw to it that the Gardens' new owners gave her free rent, free utilities, and fifty dollars a month so she could stay in her home on the grounds. She died in 1936. In the mid-1990s the Gurtler family, then Elitch's owners, bowed to economic pressures and shuttered the park. Real estate developers chopped up the land, although remnants of past glory, including the theater, remained. A new Elitch's, owned for a time by the Gurtlers, rose along the South Platte southwest of downtown.

North Denver, however, was not without fun, because it still had Lakeside, founded in 1904 and run by the Krasner family, which as late as the early twenty-first century was charging a three-dollar admission fee, providing free parking, and encouraging people to bring picnic lunches to its grounds at West Forty-Sixth Avenue and Sheridan Boulevard. Originally named White City, it was rescued from bankruptcy in the early 1930s by Benjamin Krasner. There daredevils enjoyed a heart-stopping roller coaster, while the faint of heart savored a slow trip around Lake Rhoda (named for Krasner's daughter, who has operated Lakeside for decades) on a miniature train pulled by steam engines built for the 1904 St. Louis World's Fair.

The Flip Side

With the sweet came the sour. Until the 1970s, most local historians lauded the city's rich and ballyhooed Denver's accomplishments, failing to see that it was often a coarse, brutal place. A *Rocky Mountain News* reporter, evidencing the bigotry of the times, captured some of that rawness in a December 5, 1883, article on the city's Chinese district between Fifteenth and Sixteen Streets, near Market Street, where he estimated that five hundred people lived in half a square block. He told of "outhouses overflowing into the yards. . . . [P]iles of ashes, decayed vegetables, chicken features and other refuse were piled in every corner," and he concluded that "probably no more horribly filthy location can be found anywhere in the country than in this leper spot." The "leper spot" was not, of course, to the liking of the Chinese, who found themselves trapped in such hellholes by their poverty and by the larger society's animus toward them. In the 1880s, poor Italian immigrants fared a little better than the Chinese, but still struggled to survive in shacks northwest of downtown in the Bottoms, along the South Platte River, where diphtheria and typhoid killed their children.

The town's treatment of criminals and alleged felons reflected its semibarbarous state. Andrew Green, an African American, was accused of killing Joseph Whitnah, a streetcar driver, on May 19, 1886. Tried, convicted, and sentenced to hang, Green was publicly executed July 27, 1886. A crowd estimated at twenty thousand, around 40 percent of the city's population, gathered along Cherry Creek, near its intersection with West Tenth Avenue, to witness the botched execution, which left Green twitching as he strangled. Historian William M. King in his book *Going to Meet a Man: Denver's Last Legal Public Execution, 27 July 1886,* quotes a reporter from the *Denver Tribune-Republican:* "Toddling babes were held up to view the horrible sight. Little boys clapped their hands with glee. Mothers with suckling babes looked on the scene. Now was the summer of Sheriff Cramer's delight. He had made the people happy. He had given them a spectacle equal in brutality to the exhibitions which the Roman Emperors were wont to pander to the lowest appetites of their subjects."

Eight years later, on July 25, 1894, Joseph Arata, an Italian saloonkeeper accused of killing a customer, was not even given a trial. Snatched by a mob from the Arapahoe County Jail, he was slashed, hanged, shot, dragged through downtown streets, and hanged a second time while tens of thousands watched. The *Colorado Catholic,* a Denver newspaper, aware of prejudice against Italians, observed on February 15, 1894, "No one will contend that Arata would have met the same fate had he been of a nationality other than Italian."

Intense prejudice also worked against sixteen-year-old John Preston Porter Jr., an African American, accused of raping and murdering twelve-year-old Louise Frost near Limon, Colorado, ninety miles southeast of Denver, on November 9, 1900. Arrested in Denver, Porter was tortured for four days in a sweatbox, a device police used to dehydrate and disorient prisoners. Finally threatened with the wholesale lynching of himself, his father, and his brother, he said he committed the crime. Sent to Limon, he was taken a mile and a half southeast of town, chained to an iron rail, and burned to death.

For much of its nineteenth-century history, Denver at its best was a pleasant place for its prosperous and even for its moderately situated citizens. Unfortunately, it was not always at its best, and in the 1890s things got worse, as steep declines in the price of silver triggered a depression, making the poor poorer and thrusting some of the city's wealthiest citizens into poverty. Some of them had borrowed heavily, assuming that the good times would forever roll. The 1890s taught them that gambling did not always pay.

Chapter Six

Down and Up in the 1890s

*I*n 1890 Colorado, which proudly called itself the Silver State, produced more than half the nation's silver, and as the state's chief city, Denver's fortunes were closely tied to silver. Silver kings such as Horace Tabor built buildings and speculated in real estate. The city's smelters refined silver and gold; its manufacturers and wholesale houses filled orders from mining towns; its railroads feasted on traffic to and from the mountains; its banks financed mines. But with many silver eggs in its economic basket, the city risked disaster if the market for those eggs softened. To shore up demand, Colorado congressmen in 1890 helped pass the Sherman Silver Purchase Act, which required the US Treasury to buy four and a half million ounces of silver a month at the prevailing market price. That temporarily calmed Denverites, who had nervously watched the metal's value slide as supply outstripped demand.

Crash

The Sherman Silver Purchase Act helped Denver, but it nearly bankrupted the US Treasury, as silver holders exchanged silver for gold, thereby draining national gold reserves while cramming Treasury vaults with tons of silver, which declined from $1.05 an ounce in 1890 to 82 cents by early June 1893. Nationally, Democrats and Republicans recognized that without gold reserves, the country would be hobbled, because international accounts were settled in gold. In 1892 both parties nominated presidential candidates unfriendly to silver. Democrat Grover Cleveland won, and in August 1893 he convinced Congress to repeal the Sherman Silver Purchase Act.

Even before the repeal, silver's price, sapped by slumping international demand, fell precipitously. Denverites gasped in June 1893 as the price per ounce plummeted from 82 cents to 63 cents in four days. Fearing a financial meltdown, depositors rushed to their banks to withdraw their money, only to find that their saving accounts had disappeared because bankers had loaned the money to silver kings, real estate developers, and other pillars of the community who were unable to pay it back. A dozen local banks failed in mid-July 1893, wiping out the savings of ordinary depositors. The crisis spread, as manufacturers and smelters slashed jobs. The Omaha and Grant Smelter shut down entirely for some months. The Boston and Colorado smelter at Argo kept operating because it had gold ore to refine. Home building slowed to a trickle, with only 124 houses constructed in 1894, compared to 2,000 in 1890. Soon local unemployed were joined by thousands of homeless miners who drifted down from the mountains. The city provided a camp for indigents along the South Platte River and gave them lumber so they could build boats and sail away. One group, preferring a more comfortable ride, stole a railway train, which proved unwise because authorities easily tracked them down.

Riches to Rags: The Tabors

As the unemployment rate topped 20 percent, the poor and middle class suffered greatly, but local historians have often focused their sympathies on two of the city's best-known citizens, Horace Austin Warner Tabor and his second wife, Elizabeth Doe. Tabor, a pioneer of 1859, and his first wife, Augusta, set up a general store near the future site of Leadville in the 1860s. Lucky to be present at the birth of the area's silver boom, he made a fortune, which in 1878 allowed him to move to Denver, where he bought Augusta a mansion previously owned by Henry C. Brown.

Augusta's home had spacious verandas and twenty rooms, but Horace preferred to stay at the Windsor, the city's finest hotel until the Brown Palace was built. People gossiped about his living arrangements and his liaison with a beautiful divorcée, Elizabeth McCourt Doe, known as Baby Doe. Still, his money was enough to get him appointed to a thirty-day term in the US Senate. He took advantage of his weeks in Washington, DC, to marry Elizabeth at a lavish wedding attended by President Chester Arthur. Back in Denver, he lived with her and their two children in a Capitol Hill mansion a mile south of Augusta's home.

Elizabeth "Baby Doe" Tabor, one of Colorado's most beautiful women, had an affair with silver magnate Horace Tabor. He then divorced his hardworking first wife, Augusta, to marry this beauty half his age. After Horace's death in 1899, Baby Doe clung to the Matchless Mine, near Leadville, until she met her own bitter-cold end in 1935. Courtesy History Colorado.

For her faithfulness and heartbreak, Augusta won a sizable alimony settlement that put her among the city's richest women. Unlike faithless and feckless Horace, she held on to her money until her death in 1895.

Tabor's portfolio, overly concentrated in mining and real estate, evaporated in the early 1890s, forcing him to sell practically everything. His friends rescued him by getting him appointed postmaster of Denver, so when he died on April 10, 1899, he was not dirt poor, as some writers have suggested. A legend in his own time, he got a splendid sendoff, including the honor of lying in state at the Colorado capitol. Thanks to the kindness of John Kernan Mullen and his heirs, Elizabeth hung on to the Matchless Mine, one of Horace's Leadville properties. There, at age eighty-one, she died in a cold, cluttered shack in early 1935 in the midst of another depression.

Politics, Governor Waite, and the City Hall War

The silver crisis triggered a political earthquake. Angry because national Democrats and Republicans opposed continued silver subsidies in 1892, many Coloradans abandoned the major parties and supported the People's Party of America, known as the Populist Party, which favored silver. Davis Waite, a Populist newspaper editor from Aspen, won Colorado's governorship in 1892. Waite wielded considerable power in Denver because he appointed various city boards. The police and fire departments, for example, answered to commissioners named by the governor. Seeing the police in cahoots with the underworld, the reform-minded Waite ordered the commissioners to crack down on gamblers and vice lords. When they refused, he fired them. Unwilling to accept the governor's decision, the commissioners, supported by the police and local lowlifes, including Jefferson Randolph "Soapy" Smith, barricaded themselves in the city hall at Fourteenth and Larimer Streets. Waite responded by ordering the state militia to forcibly remove the balky commissioners. On March 15, 1894, militiamen marched on city hall, where police and their underworld henchmen, bristling with guns and dynamite, prepared for battle. Bloodshed was averted, and the City Hall War ended when Waite backed down and federal troops from Fort Logan, a small army post south of the city, intervened.

Policemen and underworld denizens, including Soapy Smith, defended the Denver City Hall on March 15, 1894, against troops sent by reforming governor Davis H. Waite to clean up city government. Courtesy Denver Public Library.

Women's Suffrage

The economic and political upheaval contributed to an advance in human rights when Colorado women won the right to vote. Much of the credit for that victory rested with Denver women. In the 1880s, Caroline Churchill founded the *Queen Bee,* a newspaper dedicated to advancing women's rights. In the early 1890s, local women, including journalist Ellis Meredith, mounted a campaign to get men to agree to allow women to vote. Hoping to curry favor with women, Waite, true to his Populist principles, supported suffrage, as did many prominent Republicans. Traditional opponents, such as brewers and saloon keepers, failed to muster an effective counterattack. In November 1893, Colorado's men voted to allow women equal suffrage, and Denver gained international attention as the largest city in the United States where women could vote in all elections.

Soon Colorado had three women in its state legislature, including Clara Cressingham and Frances S. Klock from Denver. For the rest of the

In 1893 Colorado men voted for women's suffrage, making Denver the first big city in the world to enfranchise females. Courtesy History Colorado.

1890s, as historian Marcia Goldstein has documented in her University of Colorado dissertation, women actively engaged in politics but were often stymied by men intent on keeping political power. Not until 1912 when Helen Ring Robinson won a seat in the Colorado Senate was a woman elected to that chamber. Women did manage to advance their agenda by campaigning and voting for men willing to support legislation women wanted. The Women's Christian Temperance Union, led by Adrianna Hungerford, worked to restrict liquor sales. Women also successfully backed legislation to protect prostitutes from their pimps, to help orphans, and to keep juvenile offenders from being treated as adults.

Gaining the vote did not ensure women economic equality with men. Women professionals such as Ellis Meredith were rare. Most women who worked outside their own homes toiled in low-paying jobs as servants (many worked ten to fifteen hours a day), laundresses, sales ladies, and seamstresses. Emily French was typical of many single women. Forced to find a job after her husband of thirty-one years divorced her, she took work as a servant. Her diary chronicles her struggles:

[SEPTEMBER 29, 1890] Went at 7. I must go some place [*sic*] to work, we will starve sure.

[SEPTEMBER 30, 1890] Oh Dear, so hard, washed all day.

[OCTOBER 18, 1890] Up at 5, built the fire, got the breakfast.

[NOVEMBER 1, 1890] Such a week, oh Lord, the children to take care of. . . . I am so tired out. . . . [S]he [Emily's employer] let me sleep down stairs last night. I must rest, she sees that.

[NOVEMBER 9, 1890] I never combed my hair all day. I lay, for I am not feeling well enough to get up, yet I must. I come unwell last night. I am very bad of late, my age, must be.

The Capitol—Symbol of Hope

Amid the bad news of 1893 was a ray of hope, the completion that year of the exterior of the Colorado capitol. In 1868 Henry C. Brown gave Colorado ten acres on what became known as Capitol Hill as a site for a capitol building. He expected to make money by selling off his nearby property. Years passed without Colorado constructing a capitol. As Denver expanded, the vacant tract increased in value, and in 1879 Brown demanded the land back. Legal battles followed, until in 1886 the US Supreme Court ruled that Colorado could keep Brown's gift. With clear title, the state started construction in 1886 under the direction of Michigan architect Elijah E. Myers, designer of the Michigan and Texas capitols as well as the Arapahoe County Courthouse at Sixteenth Street and Court Place in Denver. He promised to design a grand edifice at a reasonable cost but spent more than anticipated, so the state fired him in 1889.

Fortunately, penny-pinching did not condemn the building to be clad in sandstone, as originally planned. Instead, granite from a quarry near Gunnison gave the capitol, long the most prominent building in Denver, a durable shell. By late 1894 enough interior work had been completed to allow the Colorado Supreme Court, Governor Davis Waite, and other officials to move in. On January 2, 1895, the Colorado General Assembly met there for the first time. Proud citizens liked the opulent building, with its interior finished in Yule marble, rare rose onyx, and oak, but they loathed its copper-sheathed dome, which got mottled and

Construction began on the Colorado capitol in 1886. As a final refinement, the dome was gilded with gold in 1908. Photo by Tom Noel.

ugly as it aged. Architect Frank E. Edbrooke and others proposed gilding the dome with thin gold foil, which was done in 1908, using two hundred ounces of Colorado gold.

Tammen, Bonfils, and Moffat

For those trapped in poverty like Emily French, Denver offered little hope. A few nimble, risk-taking capitalists, however, eyed opportunity where others saw disaster. When the *Denver Evening Post*, a small newspaper, came on the market in 1895 for $12,500, Harry Heye Tammen, a curio dealer, spotted a bargain. Without the money to buy it, he persuaded Frederick Gilmer Bonfils, a lottery operator with a dubious reputation, to provide the cash. Neither knew much about journalism. That may have been an advantage, because neither seemed constrained by old rules. They rapidly made the paper, which became the *Denver Post,* into a profitable example of what became known as yellow journalism.

Scandal sold papers, so Bonfils and Tammen harped on scandals. Gossip sold papers, so they exposed the foibles of the rich. Crusades sold papers, so they crusaded. And sometimes they did not go on crusades, if bribed not to do so. Their layout and their ethics stank, yet they attracted readers by offering them stories crafted by star writers and editors, including Damon Runyon, Gene Fowler, and George Creel. They held contests and staged events, including having magician Harry Houdini escape from a straitjacket while suspended from a flagpole in front of *Post* headquarters. They even owned a circus, Sells-Floto, which delighted the affable, roly-poly Tammen. Circulation grew and profits rose, especially since Bonfils knew how to pinch pennies.

David Halliday Moffat also emerged from the 1890s in good financial shape. He arrived in Denver in 1860 as a young man with banking knowledge he had picked up in Omaha. By 1865 he was a director of Denver's First National Bank, and in 1880 he became its president. Regarded as a safe institution during the crash of 1893, the First National weathered the storm. By 1896 it was the nation's twenty-first-largest bank, and Moffat was cashing in on the Cripple Creek gold bonanza by hauling ore on his Florence and Cripple Creek Railroad. Railroads had long been one of his passions. He backed the Denver Pacific, the city's first railroad, and the first steam engine to pull into town, on June 22, 1870, bore his name. He also served as president of the Denver and Rio Grande, the state's most important internal railroad.

In 1902, then in his sixties, Moffat embarked on an incredibly ambitious venture, the Denver Northwestern and Pacific Railroad (DNW&P, often called the Moffat Road). He proposed to build west from Denver to reach Salt Lake City, where the DNW&P could connect to California-bound tracks. The grand plan would have, in effect, created a sixth transcontinental railroad by using Denver's railroad links to the east. Plagued by winter weather and tortuous terrain, including 11,676-foot Rollins Pass, northwest of Denver, construction and operation of the DNW&P proved horrendously expensive. Moffat tried to borrow from eastern banks but wound up using his own capital and that of the First National Bank. He contemplated tunneling through the mountains but lacked the money to do what was eventually accomplished, at public expense, with the 1928 opening of the Moffat Tunnel under James Peak. He died bankrupt in 1911, leaving the bank and the fortunes of many of his associates in shambles. The DNW&P died at Craig, in northwestern Colorado, where Moffat's private railroad car, named for his daughter, Marcia, still sits.

Recovery

In an effort to break the depression, Denver initiated homegrown economic stimulus programs. Tourists had always been good for business, so in 1895 boosters organized a municipal carnival inspired by Mardi Gras in New Orleans. The Festival of Mountain and Plain featured three days of parades and exhibits showcasing Colorado's agricultural, industrial, mineral, and mercantile enterprises. At the first festival in 1895, impoverished businessmen and their wives marched in their finery, pretending to be rich as Midas. The festival lasted until 1912, long after the city had recovered.

Another booster bonanza brought longer-lasting rewards. First held in 1898, the National Western Stock Show was revived in 1906 and held annually since then, with rodeo events being added in 1931. It has become a January ritual—one of the city's best-attended and best-known attractions. The initiation and success of the Stock Show underlined a shift in the economy that, although it still drew strength from mining, especially from Cripple Creek gold, increasingly diversified, thanks to its expanding agricultural sector. The rail network that spurred the city's development as a smelting hub served it equally well as an agricultural and ranching center, with the convergence of rail lines in north-central Denver fixing the location of smelters and the nearby stockyards. If part of the price for economic recovery meant that the city risked becoming known as a cow town, it was willing to hug cows.

Home Rule

Despite the damage the depression did to many of its citizens, Denver gained ground from the slump. Contiguous suburbs saved money by consolidating with the city, thereby expanding its borders and increasing its population. Reformers, taking a cue from the nationally developing

Progressive movement, developed new schemes—ranging from reorganizing city governments to smoke abatement—for improving society. The City Hall War and state interference with local affairs fostered a home-rule movement that in 1902 led to a state constitutional amendment, giving the city considerable autonomy. Land carved from Arapahoe County allowed Denver to become the City and County of Denver, and Littleton became Arapahoe's county seat. By 1904 Denver had adopted a charter that provided for a strong mayor, and from that mayor, Robert W. Speer, came energetic leadership and a vision of Denver as Paris on the Platte.

Chapter Seven

Paris on the Platte

*E*conomic recovery, home rule, and annexations brought new opportunities. Between 1900 and 1920, the city nearly doubled its
population. As important, it used its prosperity and tax revenues to
transform itself from a drab, ugly town into a place of grace and beauty,
at least in its wealthier sections. For that Robert W. Speer, mayor from
1904 to 1912 and again from 1916 to 1918, deserves much of the credit.
Yet for all its early-twentieth-century improvements, the city remained
divided between rich and poor, infested with underworld maggots and
greedy moguls, a place where most politicians dutifully danced to tunes
whistled by powerful corporations.

Speer was a pragmatist who embraced some progressive ideas,
such as the City Beautiful movement and the building of playgrounds,
but who, at the same time, angered full-blown Progressives by doing favors for the underworld and for big corporations. He had learned the
political ropes in the corrupt 1880s, and, beholden to the system that
made him, he had little motivation to change it. Benjamin Barr Lindsey, a feisty judge, on the other hand, was an idealistic Progressive who
wanted clean government, honest elections, and upright cops. Both
Lindsey and Speer had compassion for the poor, and both backed programs to help the needy, but neither matched William Haywood, known
as "Big Bill," an energetic labor leader, in his passion for the welfare
of working people and in his belief that society needed fundamental
changes. Speer, Lindsey, and Haywood offer three windows through
which early-twentieth-century Denver may be viewed.

Robert Walter Speer

Robert W. Speer came to Denver from Pennsylvania in 1878 at the age of twenty-three. Like thousands of others, he arrived with lungs raw and bleeding from tuberculosis, under doctor's orders to seek out a dry, sunny, curative climate. Colorado's salubrious air transformed the puny Pennsylvanian. He gained weight, a strong handshake, and a broad grin. Soon he was wheeling and dealing in real estate. He turned dirt into dollars by developing a fashionable residential area snuggled up to the Denver Country Club. In this still-affluent Country Club neighborhood between East First and Fourth Avenues, from Downing Street to University Boulevard, Speer garnered his reward—his large home still stands at 300 Humboldt Street. Critics sniped that he built Speer Boulevard as a fancy driveway for himself and his Denver Country Club chums.

Speer seemed to be everywhere. As a director of the Festival of Mountain and Plain, he ballyhooed Denver. Naturally, he joined the Chamber of Commerce. Fellow optimists liked his "go-a-headativeness." They elected him president of the Denver Real Estate Exchange and named him a director of the Denver Manufacturers' Bureau. He embraced politics, becoming a darling of the Democratic Party. After election as city clerk in 1884, he moved through appointments as postmaster, Fire and Police Board commissioner, and president of the Board of Public Works. He became the city's craftiest politician. "I am a boss," Speer once confessed. "I want to be a good one."

In 1904 Speer ran for mayor after he and other city shapers drafted a new city charter, which gave the mayor great power. He won easily and quickly went to work to make Denver, as he put it, a Paris on the Platte. Although residents had been planting trees and grass for decades, hoping to transform their patch of the Great American Desert into an oasis, Speer put government muscle into their efforts by launching a tree-planting campaign that ultimately gave away 110,000 shade trees. He also established the office of the city forester to see that his plans lasted even longer than his trees. He shared his vision in a January 7, 1907, pep talk to the city council:

> We are in a plastic state. As the twig is bent so the tree will
> grow. . . . Denver can be made one of the ordinary cities of

Mayor Robert W. Speer transformed Denver from a city ugly to a city beautiful. Speer, who came to town as a youth struggling with tuberculosis, reflected in 1909, "Denver has been kind to most of us by giving to some health, to some wealth, to some happiness, and to some a combination of all. We can pay a part of this debt by making our city more attractive." Courtesy Denver Public Library.

the country, or she can be made the Paris of America. It will cost money, but this investment will pay ten dollars for every one spent. Let us start [with the Civic Center] plaza near the business center—have statues, trees, and flowers—where our people and tourists may gather each evening under the most artistic electric lighting—near the spray from grand fountains and listen to the finest music in the land. . . . Then build not an ordinary, but an extraordinary drive or Appian Way into the mountains. . . . Take these forward steps, and you will never turn back—our future greatness will be assured.

Transforming Denver

In the heart of the city, Speer proposed a gracefully landscaped Civic Center. Between the state capitol on the east and a projected new City and County Building on the west, he had some of the nation's foremost city planners design a park with monuments, a central library, fountains, and an outdoor Greek theater. The latter attracted criticism, including one local who bellyached, "What the hell do we need a Greek Theater for! We ain't got that many Greeks here!"

After the Civic Center, the second step was a network of tree-lined parkways that led from downtown to outlying residential neighborhoods. "Shaded drives," as Speer noted, "in this climate and land of bright sunshine, are appreciated more than in most cities." During hot, dry summers, parkways are at least ten degrees cooler than unshaded asphalt and cement streets. Speer Boulevard, the pacesetting parkway, also resolved the problem of what to do with dumpy, flood-prone Cherry Creek. Speer walled the creek and began landscaping it with trailing vines, shrubbery, and trees. Small triangular parks were created along Speer Boulevard where the diagonal boulevard intersected downtown streets. Two larger tracts were acquired for Sunken Gardens Park in front of West High School and Alamo Placita Park on Speer at East First Avenue. Speer Boulevard led to Washington Park via the Downing-Marion Street Parkway. East Sixth, Seventh, Seventeenth, and Monaco Parkways extended the plan into East Denver. To honor the man who made the town eyesore into the scenic centerpiece of a grand boulevard, the city council in 1910 renamed Cherry Creek Drive as Speer Boulevard.

The third step in city beautification was the establishment of large neighborhood parks to serve as mini civic centers. Although the city had started developing parks in the 1870s, Speer doubled parkland from 573 to 1,184 acres, and he promoted them as centerpieces for public buildings—schools, branch libraries, firehouses, churches, and other community hubs. Sloan's Lake, Washington, and City Parks are legacies of this plan. The mayor insisted that parks were for people to use. In one of his first steps as mayor, he ordered all "Keep Off the Grass" signs removed. At City Park, where the zoo consisted of a few chained and caged animals, Speer installed zoological gardens. Behind protective moats, monkeys, seals, and bears cavorted in spacious, natural environments. In City Park Lake, an electric fountain with nine colored lights and twenty-five water jets provided visual accompaniment to the free concerts of the Denver Municipal Band.

Realizing the special magic of water in a semiarid region, the mayor built the south lake of Washington Park and Sunken Gardens Lake and added Berkeley, Sloan's, and Rocky Mountain Lakes to the park system. Visitors found fish in the well-stocked waters as well as sailboats, canoes, and paddleboats. In winter the lakes were converted to ice-skating rinks. In an ambitious campaign to bring bathing beaches to Denver, Speer in 1911 opened a bathhouse and constructed a sandy beach on the north end of Washington Park's north lake. Similar beaches opened for the public at Berkeley, City Park, and Sloan's Lake Parks. Speer used his skill and experience as a real estate developer to the city's advantage. To secure Inspiration Point at West Forty-Ninth Avenue and Sheridan Boulevard, he bought the tract himself and then sold it and its million-dollar view of the Front Range to the city for the eight thousand dollars he had paid for it.

Whereas the private sector built clubs and amenities for the upper crust, Speer's administration constructed public tennis courts, ball fields, horseshoe pits, swimming pools, playing fields, and graciously landscaped parks and parkways. Recreational opportunities, as Progressive Era reformers argued, should not just be for the rich. Yet most of Speer's major improvements wound up in neighborhoods best described as middle class and above. Robert and Kate Speer, who had no children, made Denver's children their own. The Speers especially delighted in two statues: the Children's Fountain in City Park and *Wynken, Blynken, and Nod* in Washington Park. Playgrounds were constructed throughout the city, even in poor neighborhoods. "Three years ago," reported the magazine *American City* for May 1910, "Denver did not know that a good playground for children was something else than a vacant space where children, unsupervised, had the opportunity to fight it out. Today Denver is one of the leading cities in the playground movement."

The fourth step in the mayor's City Beautiful scheme was creation of the Denver Mountain Parks to carry public playgrounds and open space beyond the city boundaries into Clear Creek, Douglas, Jefferson, and Grand Counties. These Mountain Parks came to include the Winter Park Ski Area and the Red Rocks Outdoor Amphitheatre. Initially, they appealed to well-heeled local people who could afford automobiles, but Speer and his friends also recognized they would someday also attract out-of-state tourists and their dollars. Some 13,500 acres of Mountain Parks have inspired surrounding counties to add tens of thousands of acres of open space. Thanks to its far-flung park system, Denver is one of the few cities in the United States that boasts its own ski area, a spectacular outdoor amphitheater, and two buffalo herds.

Denver's greatest scenic asset, the mayor knew, was its view of the snowcapped Rocky Mountains—a panorama extending for more than 150 miles from Pikes Peak to the south to beyond Longs Peak on the north. While the mountains had not been growing higher, buildings and billboards had. Realizing the threat, the Speer administration urged that telegraph and telephone cables be buried underground, established a twelve-story building-height limit, and tried to ban billboards. Speer also worked with the Chamber of Commerce to fight another danger to the mountain view—Denver passed its first smoke-abatement ordinance in 1916. This early effort began the fight against air pollution that still sullies the city's reputation and mountain views.

The Municipal Auditorium

To make Denver a convention magnet, the mayor campaigned for a half-million-dollar municipal auditorium—then the largest in the nation except for Madison Square Garden in New York City. Speer and the Chamber of Commerce raised one hundred thousand dollars to celebrate the 1908 grand opening of the auditorium with the city's first national political convention. While that amount was enough to capture the Democrats in 1908, the figure was closer to a hundred million a century later, when the 2008 Democratic National Convention again focused international attention on the Mile High City.

For the 1908 convention, the city draped downtown with red, white, and blue bunting. Brass bands greeted each state delegation as it arrived at Union Station. At Union Station, arrivals were also greeted by the city's Welcome Arch. This seventy-ton bronze-coated steel gateway supported a huge "WELCOME" sign, illuminated by 2,194 lightbulbs. Initially, the arch read "WELCOME" on both the station and the downtown sides, but the Chamber belatedly realized that departing visitors should not be "WELCOME" to leave. Red-faced Chamber officials replaced that side of the sign with the word "MIZPAH." Denverites simply told visitors that it was an "Indian word" for "Howdy, pardner." Actually, *Mizpah* is the Hebrew parting salutation found in Genesis 31:49: "The Lord watch between me and thee, when we are absent one from another." To make the delegates feel even more welcome, more thousands of locals donned "I live in Denver—Ask Me" buttons and showed delegates around town. Boosters brought a trainload of snow from the mountains and dumped it in front of the auditorium so delegates could cool off with snowball fights. A band of Arapaho Indians circled downtown on a streetcar, letting out war whoops whenever they spotted a delegate. The hoopla probably brought Denver goodwill, but it failed to help the Democrats' presidential nominee, William Jennings Bryan. He lost in 1908 to William Howard Taft.

Speer, unlike Bryan, won in his race for mayor in 1908 and hence had another term to pursue his programs. He did far more than beautify parts of the city. He promoted storm sewers that made neighborhoods less flood prone. A poor section got a boon when the mayor built a bathhouse at Twentieth and Curtis Streets. There and in other bathhouses, free soap and towels allowed the unwashed masses to get washed. Although he consorted with the rich and often did their bidding, he also helped the poor. When coal prices soared in 1917, he established a city coal company to provide lignite, the poor man's low-grade coal, at a reasonable price. When bread prices rose, he proposed creating a city bakery. Speer's accomplishments rested on his power as mayor, and being mayor rested on his bossing a powerful political machine. From

Mayor Speer dedicated the WELCOME arch in front of Union Station in 1906. Mayor George Begole demolished it in 1931 as "an impediment to the automobile." With the rebirth of Lower Downtown as a popular pedestrian area, some have suggested reerecting the arch as "an impediment to the automobile." Courtesy Tom Noel Collection.

the wealthy who wanted favors from the city, including utility and transit franchises, he got campaign contributions. From saloonkeepers, brewers, and gamblers who wanted to keep reformers at bay, he got ward heelers to round up votes. Many people tolerated his machine because it worked for them and because it brought the city good things. Others, including peppery and outspoken Ben Lindsey, thought Denver was more a cesspool on the Platte than a Paris.

Benjamin Barr Lindsey

Born in Tennessee in 1869, Ben Lindsey at age eleven moved with his parents to Denver, where the family's fortunes fell. His life was almost shattered by his father's suicide, and Ben tried to kill himself, failing when his gun misfired. Work in a law firm gave him the education he needed to become an attorney, and by dabbling in politics he became a county court judge in 1900. Early in his career, he had to sentence an Italian boy convicted of stealing coal. The lad's mother unnerved Lindsey by wailing

and screaming in the courtroom. He recessed the court and investigated the case. He found "Tony" living in a squalid shack, where his father was sick with lead poisoning. The family was freezing, so the boy stole coal. That revelation set Lindsey on a crusade to treat juvenile offenders with compassion, keep them out of adult prisons, and parole them if possible. Soon the "kids judge" established a juvenile court that became a national model.

Ben Lindsey stood barely five feet tall, shorter than many of the boys he rescued with his innovative juvenile court system. Yet he stands tall among reformers for attacking the business and political corruption he called "the beast." Courtesy Denver Public Library.

At the same time, Lindsey became increasingly aware of the interconnections among vicemongers, the police, the wealthy, and the Speer machine. In 1909 Lindsey and coauthor Harvey O'Higgins published a series of articles revealing the seamy side of Denver in *McClure's*, a widely circulated national magazine. Lindsey told of wine rooms where young girls were recruited into prostitution, of inflated government contracts, of bribed jurors, of rigged elections, and of judges afraid of rocking a rotten boat. For much of that skullduggery, Lindsey blamed Speer and his henchmen. Published the next year in book form as *The Beast*, the muckraking exposé coupled with rising reform sentiment probably prompted

Speer not to run again for mayor. Reform candidate Henry Arnold won the 1912 election. In 1913 the city jettisoned its strong mayoral system and embarked on a three-year experiment with a commission form of government, a panacea touted by some progressives, in which heads of departments ran the city. Abandoning that arrangement in 1916, voters reestablished the strong mayoral system and again elected Speer mayor. Lindsey found that advocating reform was easier than getting it.

William Dudley "Big Bill" Haywood

Compared to Big Bill Haywood (220 pounds), Lindsey (110 pounds) was a reform lightweight who wanted to make minimal changes so the status quo could survive. Haywood demanded far more—a restructuring of society so workers could get their fair share of what they produced. Bathhouses were good things, but if workers were paid decently, they could afford indoor plumbing and bathtubs in their homes. Haywood was born in Salt Lake City in 1869, became a silver miner in Idaho, and by the late 1800s had joined the Western Federation of Miners (WFM). When he was elected the WFM's secretary-treasurer in 1901, he moved to Denver, where the union was headquartered. A forceful speaker, he traveled throughout the state, urging miners to demand eight-hour workdays, a minimum wage of three dollars a day, and better working conditions.

In Denver he fought for smelter men who went on strike on July 4, 1903. He fulminated against the corporations who owned the smelters. He recalled in his autobiography that he compared the homes of workers to the palatial Capitol Hill mansion of James B. Grant, one of the founders of the Omaha and Grant Smelter. "I said that a single piece of Grant's furniture would buy a dozen such houses and furniture as the strikers had. I compared the rustling silk of the wives of the smelter owners with the clatter of babies' skulls; the infant mortality rate of the smelter district was higher than in any other part of the state." Talk of babies' skulls and of workers' shanties did not amuse the "Paris on the Platte" crowd. Many men who lived in Capitol Hill mansions and whose wives wore silk rejoiced in mid-February 1906 when they learned that Haywood and other WFM officers had been kidnapped and taken to Idaho to stand trial for murdering that state's former governor. Clarence Darrow and Haywood's other attorneys convinced the jury that the case against Haywood was baseless, and so they acquitted him. When he returned to Denver on August 4, 1907, city officials turned off the "WELCOME" lights on the arch at Union Station.

Gradually gaining a national role as a leader of the Industrial Workers of the World, a militant group dedicated to workers' welfare, Haywood drifted away from Colorado after 1907. His opposition to World War I gave his enemies the ax they needed. Convicted of sedition, he fled in 1921 to the Soviet Union, where he died on May 18, 1928. Half his ashes were placed in the Kremlin's Red Square, not far from Lenin's Tomb. The other half were sent to Chicago to be buried among labor heroes. Remembered in Moscow, Haywood was largely forgotten in Denver.

Speer's Death

In 1916 citizens welcomed Speer back for a third term as mayor. His plans for more grand projects were stymied in April 1917 when the United States entered World War I. The war was still raging in early May 1918 when he walked a couple of miles to work, fed the sparrows on his office window ledge as usual, and then was stricken by the "grippe," perhaps a precursor to the influenza that ravaged the city a few months later. He died on May 14, 1918. More than ten thousand people jammed the Municipal Auditorium to say good-bye to the city's most loved and most effective leader. His widow, Kate Thrush Speer, donated part of her husband's estate of forty thousand dollars to pay for the bronze eagle and chiming clock atop Speer's dream—the City and County Building, finally completed in 1932 at the west end of the Civic Center. Kate remained in their house at 300 Humboldt Street until her death in the 1950s. Her most prized possession was a model of the *Wynken, Blynken, and Nod* statue she and Robert had erected for children in Washington Park.

Had Speer lived, the city might have better met the challenges of the next dozen years. More than a thousand of its residents died in late 1918 and early 1919 from an influenza epidemic that it could not control. In 1920 it suffered the bloodiest strike in its history. In the mid-1920s many of its citizens lapsed into Ku Klux Klan bigotry. A steady and powerful mayor, such as Speer, might have made the city's post–World War I years less painful. But that was not to be.

Chapter Eight

The Tumultuous Twenties

*A*n effigy of Kaiser Wilhelm II of Germany had a rough time in Denver on November 11, 1918, the day the Great War, later known as World War I, ended. *Municipal Facts,* a city-sponsored magazine, reported that Wilhelm was "burned at 16th and Curtis, hung to trolley poles, dragged at the tail boards of motor chariots, kicked and beaten, plastered with signs of derision, treated with a vast contempt." Throughout the day and into the night of November 11, revelers celebrated using "metal automobile rims, dishpans, anything that would make noise . . . and the din, horrible, raucous, and nerve wracking, swelled into a mighty diapason—the triumphant voice of victory." Yet at best the victory was bittersweet. A few hundred Coloradans died in the war. Far more were cut down by the horrendous influenza pandemic. Between September 1918, when the city reported its first flu fatality, and June 1919, more than fourteen hundred Denverites died.

Looking at the bright side, *Municipal Facts* proudly declared that the WELCOME arch at Union Station would "flash to our returning soldier and sailor boys a warm and tender greeting from Mother Denver that it will symbolize to them all the things that implanted in their hearts a love of their native city." The "boys" probably preferred getting a good job to tender greetings, but when they got home they found work scarce and inflation raging. If they returned with tuberculosis, they could count on good care at Fitzsimons Army Hospital in Aurora, one of the few long-lasting federal plums the Denver area got from the war. If any of the vets returned with radical political ideas, they were wise to keep their mouths shut. The community had little patience with those it considered threats. During the war, German Americans felt the jingoistic sting of

100 percent Americans, so local Germans sensibly adapted by keeping a low profile and getting rid of German names—the German American Trust Company morphed into the American Bank and Trust Company, and the Kaiserhof Hotel became the Kenmark. Libraries threw out their German books, and schools stopped teaching German. After the war the Russian Revolution triggered a Red Scare in the United States, and Denver, like much of the rest of the country, searched for Communists but found only a few.

Postwar inflation posed more of a threat than did radicals. Between 1916 and 1919, food prices rose by 41 percent and the cost of clothes by 60 percent. Many people, unable to increase their income, saw their savings and their purchasing power eroded. Denver Tramway Company employees, however, had hope. They were unionized, and before automobiles became commonplace most people depended on the tramway's trolleys for transportation. In 1919 streetcar drivers successfully struck to prevent a wage cut. In 1920 they asked for a pay increase that the company refused. On Sunday, August 1, more than nine hundred drivers walked off the job.

The company quickly replaced strikers with strikebreakers, who wrapped the streetcars in wire mesh and armed them with canisters filled with soapsuds. Strikers rushed the cars, derailed some, burned some, and beat strikebreakers. On August 5, 1920, strikers attacked tramway headquarters at Fourteenth and Arapahoe Streets and later that day stormed the *Denver Post*'s offices in retaliation for that paper's supporting the company. There they smashed windows, tried to set fires, and rolled newsprint down Champa Street. Frederick Bonfils, the *Post's* copublisher, stayed in his mansion at East Tenth Avenue and Humboldt Street, protected by armed guards on the roof. As violent as the strikers were, however, they did not come close to matching the brutality of the strikebreakers, who killed seven people, all of them merely bystanders. Federal troops restored order. The strike was broken, and so was the drivers' union.

The reactionary forces that brutally put down the tramway strike strongly influenced Denver for the ensuing quarter century. Progressive ideals, which had briefly flowered between 1900 and 1917, occasionally resurfaced but usually did not last. Many feared unions, fretted about

Inequities between rich and poor led to labor strife, such as the 1920 Denver Tramway workers' strike, during which strikers overturned scab-driven trolleys in front of the Cathedral of the Immaculate Conception. Courtesy Tom Noel Collection.

radicals, and fussed about crime. Practically everyone worried about disease. Might another flu epidemic sweep the city? Would TB continue to slowly consume thousands? The smallpox epidemic of 1921–22, which killed more than two hundred, added fuel to underlying fears. Many Denverites looked for scapegoats and found them in people who deviated from a hypothetical norm that might loosely be described as white, English-speaking, native-born, and Protestant. The others supposedly were not 100 percent American and hence were seen as dangerous. During World War I, German Americans bore the brunt of that bigotry. During the Red Scare, foreigners living in Globeville and other smelter neighborhoods became targets. During the flu epidemic, health authorities complained about foreigners who failed to obey health regulations, implying that they were a menace to everyone. Crime could also be blamed on the foreign born. Were those Italians in North Denver making wine and selling it?

Of crime the city had its fair share. When Philip S. Van Cise, a former World War I lieutenant colonel, won election as district attorney in 1920, he had a police captain give him a tour of the underworld. He found gambling, prostitution, and illegal drinking flourishing. Colorado had banned liquor manufacturing and liquor sales in saloons and stores in 1916, four years before national Prohibition went into effect, but laws did not stop drinking. For breaking the rules, some were severely punished and others were not. Judge Ben Lindsey's papers at the Library of Congress include grand-jury testimony he gave in October 1921 in which he railed against unequal application of Prohibition laws. Poor, young, and foreign-born people went to jail for small transgressions. Lindsey complained that rich scofflaws, such as Henry M. Blackmer, an oilman who gained notoriety for his role in the Teapot Dome scandal of the mid-1920s, could circumvent the law by secretly filling their cellars with liquor and then serving it to guests or taking a nip themselves. Because they did not charge their friends for a drink and because state law did not allow search warrants unless liquor was sold, the rich could and did drink freely. Lindsey suggested that the jailing of one wealthy violator "would do more to discourage bootlegging in this community than the jailing of all the small fry among the foreign class that are mostly brought into court."

Rise of the Ku Klux Klan

Lindsey's solution was not Denver's solution. Instead, tens of thousands joined the Ku Klux Klan, a fear-based organization that claimed to be full of virtue and tough on crime. Originally founded in the post–Civil War South to keep African Americans from exercising their civil rights, the Klan was resurrected in Georgia in 1915. Its updated list of "undesirable" Americans included Roman Catholics and Jews as well as blacks. The secretive group, whose male members wore white robes with pointed hoods, spread to the North, Midwest, and West, first reaching Denver in 1922. It grew rapidly, and, despite the opposition of such figures as district attorney Philip Van Cise, by 1923, under the leadership of grand dragon John Galen Locke, it was a force in Denver politics. Locke had come to Denver as a teenager and eventually graduated from a homeopathic medical school. Apparently, he was not personally particularly prejudiced against Catholics and Jews. His attorney was Jewish, and two of his secretaries were Catholic. Some of his followers were, no doubt, like him—joiner types who saw social, political, and financial advantages to belonging to a big organization.

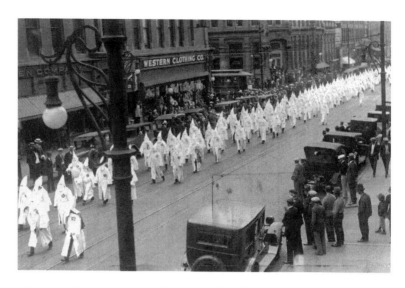

Many Denverites joined the Klan, which posed as a reform group intent on controlling crime. Here the Klan parades down Sixteenth Street. Courtesy Denver Public Library.

Benjamin Franklin Stapleton, a leftover from the Speer political machine, ran for mayor in 1923. A Kentucky native, he had served as a judge and as the city's postmaster. His election in 1923 rested in part on his disavowal of secret societies and in part on his secret membership in the Klan. He was the ultimate stealth candidate—a man who seemingly opposed the Klan while being a part of it. Within a year, however, he was in trouble, as anti-Klan Denverites fumed when he gave Klansmen key city jobs. In 1924 anti-Klan forces tried to remove him by holding a recall election. To save his political hide, Stapleton openly embraced the Klan, and the organization helped him survive the recall.

Blacks constituted less than 3 percent of the city's population in the 1920s. Compared to blacks in many other parts of the country, they were moderately prosperous. Their literacy rate exceeded 90 percent, and more than a third were homeowners. Concentrated in an area near East Twenty-Sixth Avenue and Welton Street known as Five Points, they were segregated from the rest of the city. They could swim at Curtis Park Pool, north of Five Points, but not on the same days as whites. They could attend shows at the Tabor Theater downtown but could sit only in the balcony. They could purchase homes in the Five Points neighborhood, but when their population grew and they wished to move farther east toward City Park, they faced brutal resistance.

Mistreatment of African Americans began well before the Klan came to town. The Klan simply capitalized on already existing white biases and used them as a recruiting tool to gain members. The same can be said of its emphasizing deep anti-Semitic and anti-Catholic attitudes born of centuries of European history. The Klan demonized Catholics as un-American puppets of the pope in Rome who some said wanted to make Colorado his summer home. The Klan cast Jews as foreigners, enemies of Christians, as Christ killers.

Klan scare tactics included burning crosses, staging parades, and holding mass meetings at the Cotton Mills Stadium, near West Evans Avenue and Santa Fe Drive, and atop South Table Mountain, which towers over Golden. Rumor had it that some Kluxers contemplated dynamiting the Roman Catholic Cathedral of the Immaculate Conception, but Locke supposedly dissuaded hotheads by telling them the Catholics had considerable insurance on the building and would rebuild an even grander church.

For all their rhetoric and posturing, the local Klan, which grew to an estimated twenty-five thousand or more male members, with additional thousands in the women's Klan, was timid when it came to violence. They were bold, however, when it came to politics and to boycotts. Locke and other Klan leaders wanted power and money, and they saw the Klan as an avenue to both. Politicians controlled jobs. When Stapleton made Klansman William Candlish chief of police, Catholic policemen found themselves in danger of losing their jobs. When the Klan helped elect Klansman Clarence Morley governor of Colorado in 1924, political plums went to Klansmen. Klan members boycotted Catholic merchants and capitalized on their hatred of Catholics by selling a cigar named the CYANA, an acronym for "Catholic You Are Not American." To attract Klan patronage, businesses concocted cute ads such as the Universal Wet Wash's "Klean Klothes for Kiddies" and Gano Senter's Kool Kozy Kafe.

Many bowed before the Klan. The *Rocky Mountain News* supported it, and the *Denver Post,* whose reactionary stances fueled Klan ideology, vacillated. District attorney Philip Van Cise opposed the Kluxers, as did

John Galen Locke, a short, fat physician, founded and spearheaded the Denver Ku Klux Klan as grand dragon. Courtesy Denver Public Library.

Ben Lindsey. In a November 3, 1924, letter, Lindsey told of a meeting where "wild, fanatical women like maniacs hissed in my face, 'You dirty cur,' etc." The little judge asked "one of the infuriated creatures" why she called him a cur. "With a demonical laugh, she screamed, 'You are not 100% American. You are against the Klan.'"

Klan Downfall

The Klan reached its high-water mark in 1924, when it saved Ben Stapleton from recall, elected Clarence Morley governor, and put Rice Means, a Klansman, in the US Senate. The magnitude of its triumph, however, was matched by the speed of its downfall. Ironically, the Klan's destruction came not from its avowed foes such as Ben Lindsey or Philip Van Cise, but from one of its most powerful allies—bland, bespectacled Ben Stapleton. By early 1925, he had soured on the hooded bigots, probably because he did not want to take orders from Locke and because he realized that some in the organization were far from the holy upholders of civic virtue they claimed to be. He recognized that some Klansmen drank and gambled, and he knew that the Klan-controlled police department was hobnobbing with the underworld.

Stapleton wanted to expose that unholy alliance but could not use the corrupt police department to do it. So he skillfully and secretly recruited honest cops, members of the American Legion (a veterans organization), and state policemen to make a strike force of around 130 men. For three months they planned their campaign. On Good Friday, April 10, 1925, Stapleton's little army raided speakeasies, brothels, and gambling dens, and in subsequent weeks they repeated the procedure. As the dust cleared, it became obvious that the Klan was not upholding Christian virtues. Locke's troubles multiplied when in May he was charged with income tax invasion. In June the national Klan organization moved to oust him. He resigned as grand dragon in July, by which time thousands of his followers were converting their robes into pillowcases. Klan embers smoldered for years. The Denver women's chapter, renamed the Colorado Cycle Club, sputtered out of existence in 1945. But as an organized political force capable of swaying elections, the Denver Klan was dead by 1926.

The Klan's collapse did not mean that white Protestants started treating Catholics, blacks, and Jews with decency and respect. Old prejudices remained strong. Blacks and Jews were barred from most neighborhoods by restrictive real estate covenants until the late 1940s, and even after that custom controlled the makeup of most parts of the city. When blacks tried to swim at Washington Park in South Denver in mid-August 1932, they were driven out by a white mob. It was not until the late 1960s that the city

Washington Park's north lake offered this sandy beach until fear of polio closed it in the 1950s. Whites considered it their turf and drove blacks away in 1932 when they tried to integrate the beach. Courtesy Denver Public Library.

reluctantly began to take school integration seriously. One Catholic, William McNichols Sr., stitched together a political coalition that allowed him to be consistently elected city auditor, but other Catholics found it hard until the late 1950s to win major political offices.

John Galen Locke died of a heart attack on April Fools' Day in 1935 and was buried in an impressive mausoleum in Fairmount Cemetery, a granite fortress that federal agents had stormed in the 1920s to see if the dragon was hiding his financial records there.

Ben Lindsey lost his judgeship and was disbarred in Colorado. His friends saw that as a vindictive attempt on the part of his many enemies to destroy him. His enemies considered it fit punishment for a gadfly who had stung them for decades. Lindsey moved to California, where officials ignored his Colorado disbarment. There he served as a Los Angeles Superior Court judge until 1943, when he died of a heart attack. His wife, Henrietta, brought some of his ashes back to Denver, where she scattered them near Sixteenth Street and Tremont Place at the site of the by then razed courthouse where Lindsey had held court for more than a quarter century.

The year Lindsey died, Ben Stapleton won his fourth term as mayor. The political acumen he showed in the 1920s served him for most of the rest of his life, as did the vote-getting machine he built based on city patronage. For his success he could also thank luck. He lost the mayor's job in 1931, which kept him out of office during the early years of the Great Depression, sparing him from dealing with and perhaps taking the blame for some of the worst years in the city's economic history.

Chapter Nine

This Thing Called Depression

For decades Louise Hill, daughter-in-law of smelter king Nathaniel Hill, reigned as the grande dame of high society from her Georgian mansion at 969 Sherman Street in the most fashionable part of Capitol Hill. In her midsixties in the early 1930s, she should have been able to kick off her slippers and relax. But as her papers, preserved at History Colorado's Stephen Hart Library, reveal, she had worries. She wrote her son Nathaniel, "The stock market is so depressing; there is nothing to do or say. I could not think of going to Europe, of course, in the first place, there is no one in Paris, I hear. I don't intend to buy any new clothes— just wear my old ones—So there is not much use in my going to Europe, is there."

For Louise and her neighbors on Capitol Hill, the stock market crash of October 1929 came as a shock and a threat. Charles Boettcher stayed awake nights worrying about the capital he had tied up in the American Beet Sugar Company. Charles's son, Claude, walloped by Wall Street, borrowed millions of dollars, using his life insurance as collateral. Then he plunged back into stocks at a low point and recouped at least part of his fortune. With deep pockets, Hill and the Boettchers could ride out hard times. Claude celebrated New Year's Eve of 1930 at his home at East Eighth Avenue and Logan Street (now the Colorado governor's official residence) with seventy-five friends who at midnight watched as artificial silver rain floated down on the mansion's grounds. Louise Hill wrote a friend in July 1931, "Denver is exactly the same, everybody giving a party every day."

Temporarily, Louise was correct. The full force of the Depression did not hit the city until late 1931. Between 1929 and 1931, the value of Colorado's industrial products declined from $306 million to $184 million.

Farmers raked in $213 million in 1929, but earned only $82 million in 1932. In western Colorado orchard owners let peaches rot when the prices they were offered would not pay the cost of picking the fruit. Potato growers in the San Luis Valley did the same thing. As the state's fortunes sank, so did Denver's. Banks unable to collect on their loans went broke. The Italian-American Bank defaulted, thereby wiping out savings poor people had acquired over a lifetime. When the First National Bank of Aurora failed, its president admitted that he had been falsifying its books for eight years. By 1932 the local unemployment rate, although not precisely measured, probably stood at 25 percent. Hoping that Charles Boettcher would take pity on her, Jennette Beresford, a widow, begged for help in a May 12, 1932, letter preserved in the Boettcher Papers at the Stephen Hart Library: "Within the last three years—a bank failure—a motor accident—long severe illness of my son, and this thing called depression. Now we are really quite hungry."

Beresford had to beg because between 1931 and 1933, local and state social safety nets, meager in the best of times, broke down, as governments and private charities ran out of money. A few blocks west of the state capitol, the Reverend Edgar M. Wahlberg stank up Grace Methodist Church making sauerkraut to feed the hungry. Thousands of people associated with the Unemployed Citizens League traded their labor for farm produce, renovated buildings to use as homeless shelters, baked bread, ran soup kitchens, and repaired shoes. On the banks of the South Platte, men and women panned for gold, hoping to make a few dollars. Homeless people slept in zebra stalls, lion cages, and elephant barns once used by the animals of the Sells-Floto Circus at West Thirty-Eighth Avenue and Hazel Court. Others squeezed into shacks along the South Platte River. Near Santa Fe Drive and West Alameda Avenue, hundreds lived in tents provided by the Colorado National Guard.

City leaders, including George D. Begole, who replaced Ben Stapleton as mayor in 1931, pressured by Claude Boettcher and others, hesitated to raise taxes. In fact, governments and schools, like the private sector, cut costs, thereby compounding the problem. Still, the city provided some succor. It let the destitute sleep in the old city hall at Fourteenth and Larimer Streets. With federal help, it provided subsistence doles to nearly twelve thousand families, one of every seven households. By the end of 1933, Denver was facing bankruptcy, and the federal government was threatening to end its subsidies unless the state of Colorado bore part of the burden. With an estimated forty thousand needing aid, some feared riots.

Franklin D. Roosevelt's New Deal to the Rescue

Denver looked to the federal government for help, especially after Franklin D. Roosevelt became president on March 4, 1933. He offered a "New Deal," and within a hundred days of taking office he stabilized the banking system and launched relief programs. One of the largest, the Federal Emergency Relief Administration (FERA), promised to provide jobs, but asked the states to shoulder a small part of the cost. Legislators refused to do that during 1933. Late in the year, the federal government said it would cut off funds if the state did not ante up. When the Colorado General Assembly convened in early 1934, relief seekers converged on the capitol and, by some accounts, scared legislators away and sat in their chairs. The *Nation,* a national magazine, described the hullabaloo in its February 7, 1934, issue as "the first Communist meeting to be held under the dome of any state capitol in the United States." Edgar Wahlberg saw the ruckus differently. In his book *Voices in the Darkness,* he remembered, "There were catcalls and jeers from the galleries as these people were finally confronted with the representatives. . . . There was not a single instance of meanness. People returned to their homes as quietly as they had come, but with new hope." The hope was justified, as the general assembly raised the gasoline tax to provide matching funds for relief.

FERA and its successor, the Works Progress Administration (WPA), hired thousands to work on mainly small-scale projects such as improving parks, conducting historical interviews, making mattresses, and improving streets. At the State Historical Society of Colorado, unemployed architects crafted a scale-model diorama of Denver in 1860. The Federal Writers Project compiled a state guidebook. The Federal Theater Project hired actors and produced plays. It even employed a sword swallower. One aspiring local playwright, Mary Coyle Chase, persuaded the Federal Theater, located at 1447 Lawrence Street, to produce her play *Me Third,* which went to New York as a Broadway play retitled *Now You've Done It.* It fizzled, but Chase bounced back by writing *Harvey,* a comedy that won the 1945 Pulitzer Prize for Drama. Artists won federal commissions to paint murals, such as Frank Mechau's *Horses at Night* for the Denver Public Library and Boardman Robinson's *Colorado Stock Sale* in the Englewood Post Office. US Treasury Department officials in Washington, DC, asked Robinson to reflect the history of the community. He replied in a letter preserved in the Public Building Administration Records in the National Archives, "There is no history of this Denver suburb of Englewood, but the thrilling saga of real estate exploitation." With federal backing, Gladys Caldwell carved two Rocky Mountain sheep that still grace the south entrance to the federal courthouse at Eighteenth and Stout Streets.

George E. Cranmer, who became manager of parks and improvements when Benjamin Stapleton returned as mayor in 1935, used federal agencies to create a lasting legacy at Red Rocks west of the city. Denver purchased the spectacular rocks at the base of Mount Morrison in 1928,

The Colorado History Museum, now History Colorado at 1200 Broadway, used New Deal federal funding to hire unemployed historians and artists to construct dioramas, including this 1860 model of Denver. Courtesy History Colorado.

In the late 1930s, Civilian Conservation Corps and Works Progress Administration workers transformed giant foothills rock formations into Red Rocks Amphitheatre. Among many nationally prominent groups to play Red Rocks is the Mormon Tabernacle Choir, shown here. Courtesy Denver Public Library.

including the surrounding 1,640 acres for the Denver Mountain Parks system. Cranmer, who had visited a Roman amphitheater at Taormina in Sicily, recognized that Denver too could have an outdoor theater with superb acoustics by putting seating between two of the gigantic jutting sandstone slabs. Architect Burnham Hoyt designed the amphitheater to accommodate ten thousand. Cranmer used young men employed by the Civilian Conservation Corps, another New Deal agency, and WPA labor to build it. Completed in 1941, the Red Rocks Amphitheatre remains today a venue attracting national and international stars.

Water and Other Large Projects

The federal government made billions available to states and cities for large projects, which often required matching local funds. Denver was willing to put up the money in order to get what it had always struggled to get—water. Gold-rush pioneers on the banks of Cherry Creek dug wells to tap groundwater, only to find that they lowered the water table and soon had to dig deeper or seek supplies elsewhere. Capitalists organized water companies. James Archer constructed Lake Archer on the South Platte, a couple of miles south of the city center. Citizens hoped in the early 1880s that deep artesian wells could supply them with pure drinking water, but that supply proved inadequate. In the 1890s, Walter Scott Cheesman and other investors reached forty miles southwest of the city to build Cheesman Dam (completed in 1905) to impound South Platte water. In 1918 the city purchased the privately owned Denver Union Water Company and gave the Denver Water Board (DWB), a new government agency, the job of supplying water. With help from the federal government in the mid-1930s, the DWB completed the first large diversion of western slope water to Denver through the Pioneer Bore of the Moffat Tunnel. For the rest of the twentieth century and into the twenty-first, fetching water was to be one of the metro area's greatest challenges, involving money, politics, and engineering.

Providing safe water, especially to users north of the city, also bedeviled Denver, which dumped its sewage into the South Platte, thereby sickening downstream drinkers. Thanks to a grant from the Public Works Administration (PWA), the city built a $3.4 million sewage disposal plant. The PWA helped fund a new police headquarters at 1245 Champa

Street and supplied part of the money for a marble-clad state office building at East Fourteenth Avenue and Sherman Street. In Aurora federal dollars paid for the giant Fitzsimons Army Hospital. Unfortunately, from Denver's standpoint, it completed its massive 435-foot-long, four-story City and County Building on Bannock Street between West Colfax and Fourteenth Avenues in 1932 before PWA money was available.

Boettcher, Bonfils, and Brown

The Great Depression defined the 1930s, but it was not the only headline grabber. For weeks the kidnapping of Charles Boettcher II, the adult son of Claude and grandson of Charles, trumped all the stories of the Depression. Taken late at night from the garage of his home at 777 Washington Street on February 12, 1933, Charles II was blindfolded and whisked away. His abductors demanded sixty thousand dollars for his release. Police and four thousand volunteers searched Denver, while the kidnappers hid the purloined plutocrat on a turkey ranch in South Dakota. The Boettchers paid the ransom, and Charles was released on March 1. Supposedly, the gang, led by Verne Sankey, had originally planned on kidnapping *Denver Post* publisher Frederick Bonfils while he walked his poodle in Cheesman Park. Bonfils unwittingly outwitted the outlaws by dying before they could snatch him.

Bonfils's death in February 1933 and that of Margaret Tobin Brown (often referred to as Molly) in October 1932 deprived the city of two of its most colorful characters. Bonfils died in his early seventies, rich and powerful in his palatial home. Brown died in her midsixties with only a remnant of her money in a New York hotel room. In ensuing decades, her fame grew and his faded.

Bonfils and his partner, Harry H. Tammen, who died in 1924, purchased the *Denver Post* in 1895 and made it the city's most read, profitable, and feared newspaper. The affable Tammen, who left much of his fortune to Children's Hospital, was liked. Egotistical, mercurial, and tough, Bonfils was appreciated by some and hated by others. In August 1932, Walter Walker, editor of the *Grand Junction Sentinel* in western Colorado, described Bonfils to a Denver gathering as a "vulture," a "contemptible dog," and "a public enemy [who] has left the trail of a slimy serpent across Colorado for thirty years." The *Rocky Mountain News* published Walker's fulmination, which prompted Bonfils to sue the *News* for libel. Philip S. Van Cise, the *News*'s attorney, adopted a two-pronged defense strategy. First, he set out to show that Bonfils's reputation was so low that nothing Walker said could detract from it. Van Cise found that easy—over the years others had called Bonfils, among other things, a "cootie-covered rat," a "polecat," and the "devil's paramour." Van Cise also hired a private detective to pry into Bonfils's private life. Bonfils, stressed by the fear that Van Cise would reveal a checkered past, was unable, in a day before antibiotics, to recover from an ear infection that killed him on February 2, 1933. By subterfuge, the *Rocky Mountain News* learned of his death before the *Post* did and hence had the delight of first reporting the passing of its great competitor.

Stories about Bonfils's life and death occupied almost the whole front page of the *Denver Post* on Thursday evening, February 2. The passing of Margaret Tobin Brown in New York City received less attention in Denver, where she had lived on and off since 1894 when she and her husband, James J., came down from Leadville, where he had made a modest fortune in gold mining. They purchased a home at 1340 Pennsylvania Street, a substantial place with room for servants. She stuffed the home with furniture, bric-a-brac, and a polar-bear rug. Margaret, like many other suddenly well-heeled women, wanted to prance with the social set but sometimes found her way blocked because she was Irish and Roman Catholic. Her fondness for ostentatious clothes and furs also worked against her. Caroline Bancroft, one of Brown's biographers, reports that cruel people referred to her as "Colorado's unique fur-bearing animal." She was, it seems, not welcome at Louise Hill's card parties, although Catholics appreciated her as an organizer of charity events. Aboard the *Titanic* when it sank on April 15, 1912, Brown survived and later raised money to aid victims and their families. She capitalized on the tragedy for years, proclaiming that she was "unsinkable." Yet she would have slipped into the shadows of history, as Bonfils and Tammen did, if Meredith Willson had not refloated her in his Broadway musical *The Unsinkable Molly Brown* (1960), which led to a 1963 movie of the same title. The buoyancy of her myth was further ensured in 1971 when Historic Denver, Inc., a preservation organization, purchased her Pennsylvania Street home and turned it into a popular tourist attraction.

Although the Depression, crime, kidnapping, and occasional dust storms cast a pall over the 1930s, the city enjoyed some bright days. On May 26, 1934, in a test run, the Burlington Railroad's Denver Zephyr raced from Denver to Chicago in a little more than thirteen hours, clocking top speeds of more than 110 miles an hour. In 1936 the sleek, stainless-steel diesel Zephyr began regular service between Denver and Chicago, cutting travel time from twenty-four to around sixteen hours, allowing passengers to reach the Windy City overnight. George Cranmer, the city's manager of parks and improvements, saw that speedy trains could benefit the tourist industry, which suffered from seasonal imbalance, with many tourists from the Midwest and East in the summer and far fewer in the winter. He hoped to attract winter visitors by developing a railroad-accessible ski area near the city. Already ski enthusiasts had discovered an ideal location in Winter Park on the western side of the Moffat Tunnel. There the Civilian Conservation Corps and volunteer labor created ski slopes. In early 1938, trains from Denver began bringing skiers to Winter Park, but it was not until more than a quarter century later that jet airplanes and the building of Interstate 70 into the mountains made Cranmer's dream of winter tourists into a full-blown and profitable reality.

Margaret "Molly" Brown, a poor Irish girl, is celebrated for her *Titanic* heroics, philanthropic endeavors, and championing of feminist and reform causes. Her Denver house is now a popular museum. Courtesy Denver Public Library.

New Deal Sunset

The New Deal kept many people working and tremendously benefited Denver and the state by constructing buildings, roads, sewage plants, and water projects. Still, many Denverites wished they did not have to accept relief jobs. By 1939 economic skies were sunnier than they had been in 1933, and they became even brighter in the early 1940s, as Uncle Sam poured billions of dollars into local war industries. With millions of men serving as soldiers and sailors, the demand for labor soared. Women, blacks, and Hispanics, whose job prospects were bleak during the 1930s, found jobs. By 1942 the Depression was dead.

Chapter Ten

World War II and the Postwar Boom

*W*ar is hell for people whose lives, families, and fortunes are destroyed by it, but for most Denverites World War II brought prosperity and full employment, including jobs for women and minorities. After the war federal defense dollars continued to flow, making the "good" war the most transformative event in the city's history since the 1859 gold rush.

Military Installations and War Industries

Well before the United States entered World War II on December 8, 1941, Denver boosters were corralling defense dollars. During World War I, they persuaded the US Army to build Fitzsimons Hospital in Aurora. Opened in 1918 as a haven for tuberculosis patients, it became a general hospital that opened the state's largest building early in December 1941 in time to treat some of the first World War II casualties. After the army closed Fitzsimons in 1999, the main hospital building remained, and the spacious site became a magnet for medical facilities, including the University of Colorado's Anschutz Medical Campus.

In the mid-1930s, the city raised $750,000 to buy the Agnes Phipps Memorial Sanatorium and surrounding land at Sixth Avenue and Quebec Street for Lowry Air Base, a US Army Air Force facility initially used to train aerial photographers. Hundreds of thousands of military personnel cycled through the base before it closed in 1994. Known nationally in the 1950s because it served as President Dwight Eisenhower's summer White House while he vacationed in Colorado (1953–55) and because it housed the Air Force Academy from 1955 to 1958, Lowry could also boast of having the first Titan 1 intercontinental ballistic missile (ICBM) silos, holes in the ground more than 160 feet deep, located on the base's bombing

Fitzsimons Hospital, constructed in 1941, is now the centerpiece of the multibillion-dollar Anschutz Medical Campus in Aurora, which includes the University of Colorado Health Sciences Center, University Hospital, Children's Hospital, Veterans Hospital, and a Bio-Science Complex. Photo by Tom Noel.

range east of Aurora. Citizens welcomed the dollars and prestige Lowry brought but fretted about having huge airplanes flying over their neighborhoods. The September 29, 1943, crash of a B-24 in South Denver, near East Yale Avenue and Marion Street, made the danger obvious. Seven crewmen died, but property damage was light in what was then a largely undeveloped part of town. Two crashes in December 1951 and one in 1956 took additional lives, destroyed homes, and brought demands that Lowry transfer its flight operations farther east to Buckley Field in Aurora, which it did by the mid-1960s.

Fort Logan, established southwest of the city in 1887, was until the early 1940s a minor post. Its soldiers helped quell the 1894 City Hall War, fought in the 1898 Spanish-American War, and restored order in the wake of the 1920 streetcar strike. During the Depression it housed a Civilian Conservation Corps camp. Its glory days came during World War II, when it morphed into a clerical training center for the US Army Air Force. After 1945 Fort Logan faced a bleak future until resurrected as a national cemetery. When aviator Harry Miller died in China in 1944, the army went to great lengths to recover his remains but had no national cemetery in Colorado in which to bury him. His mother, Kathrien, lobbied hard to get unused acreage at Fort Logan made into hallowed ground, and with the help of veterans' organizations and Denver's US congressman John A. Carroll, she succeeded. Harry was interred at Fort Logan National Cemetery in 1950, the year it opened.

During World War II, the city feasted on defense jobs. Steelworks prefabricated ships that went to California for assembly. At the Denver Municipal Airport (later renamed Stapleton), thousands of workers modified B-17 and B-29 bombers to make them more deadly. At East Thirty-Eighth Avenue and York Street, the army built a half-million-square-foot medical supply depot. The Denver Ordnance Plant, located west of the city on West Sixth Avenue and Kipling Street, employed nearly twenty thousand munitions makers at its production peak in 1943. After the war, the complex became home to the Denver Federal Center, which included federal agencies such as the Bureau of Reclamation, the United States Geological Survey, the Bureau of Land Management, and the General Services Administration. At the Rocky Mountain Arsenal, situated on nearly twenty thousand acres northeast of the city, chemists and other workers brewed poison gas and napalm. After the war, the army continued to make poison gas there, while private companies manufactured pesticides and other chemical concoctions. When ten bomblets filled with the deadly nerve gas Sarin cropped up in a waste dump in 2000, the public was unnerved. After cleanup much of the tract was made into the Rocky Mountain Arsenal Wildlife Refuge, home to bison, eagles, owlets, and many other creatures unfazed by the arsenal's toxic past.

Home-front patriots helped win the war in other ways. They collected scrap rubber, saved fat that was used to make munitions, and gathered scarce tin and copper. They puttered in backyard Victory Gardens and endured rationing of meat, sugar, butter, rubber, and other commodities. Some slept in bunk beds in spare rooms, basements, and attics, because there was virtually no nonmilitary housing constructed during the conflict. They made do with old cars and public transportation because there were no new cars to be had. Price controls kept a lid on inflation. With consumer goods in short supply, citizens saved their money and loaned much of it to Uncle Sam by buying more than a half-billion dollars' worth of US savings bonds. And they sent tens of thousands of their sons and daughters into war, from which more than eight hundred from the Denver metro area did not come back, including Major General Maurice Rose, son of a Denver rabbi and namesake of General Rose Hospital.

Postwar National Defense: Martin and Rocky Flats

Crowds jammed downtown to celebrate Japan's surrender in mid-August 1945, but the hoopla could not erase fears that the war's end might end wartime prosperity, as had happened after World War I. Historians now see those concerns as exaggerated. Soldiers and sailors were anxious to return home, get married, and start families. Pent-up demand for housing, automobiles, refrigerators, washers, nylons, television sets after the city got TV in mid-1952, and a universe of playthings coupled with money stashed in savings accounts and bonds triggered a gusher of spending and prosperity. Cold War and hot war defense needs (Korea, Vietnam, Iraq, and Afghanistan) ensured that the military-industrial juggernaut launched in World War II would roll on into the twenty-first century. Some veterans took advantage of their educational benefits to earn degrees at the University of Denver, the University of Colorado, and Regis College. Many airmen once stationed at Lowry liked Colorado's climate and its mountains, so some returned after the war, as did defense workers.

Savvy boosters kept fishing for defense dollars. In the 1950s, they landed two whales, one that might have destroyed much of the metropolitan area, the other a more benign sugar daddy. When the Glenn L. Martin Company began building Titan I ICBMs in Waterton Canyon, southwest of Denver, in the mid-1950s, no one could have predicted that fifty years later it (by then Lockheed Martin Space Systems) would partner with Boeing to form United Launch Alliance, which produced Atlas V rockets, using components from Russia, to launch missions to study Mars and space beyond Pluto. Driven by defense dollars, Martin and its successors made Denver an aerospace hub and with numerous other space, aviation, and defense companies—Jeppesen, Northrup Grumman, Raytheon, and Sierra Nevada, to name a few—pumped billions of dollars into Front Range communities.

The aerospace industry has rocketed into prominence in the Denver region. Lockheed Martin Space Systems in Littleton, one of the largest firms, has manufactured many spacecraft, including this Titan IV missile. Courtesy Tom Noel Collection.

Rocky Flats, sixteen miles northwest of Denver, also drew out Cold War fears in the early 1950s, but unlike Martin it eventually died, to the great relief of those who feared it as one of the most dangerous places on earth. Its workers made around seventy thousand plutonium triggers for hydrogen bombs, and that plutonium, besides poisoning some of those laborers, came uncomfortably close to making a radioactive wasteland of much of the metropolitan area. Journalist Len Ackland, in *Making a Real Killing: Rocky Flats and the Nuclear West,* recounted the fire of May 11, 1969: "If the fire had burned through Building 776–777's already softening roof, thousands of pounds of deadly plutonium in the form of powdery ash would have exposed hundreds of thousands . . . living nearby to toxic radiation." As a precautionary measure, the plant added additional buffer acreage. Peace activists occasionally demonstrated there, but it took the end of the Cold War to convince Uncle Sam to close the facility, which for a good part of its life was run by the Dow Chemical Company. After it ceased operations in 1992, it kept employing people for more than a decade in a multi-billion-dollar cleanup program that included tearing down eight hundred buildings. Eventually, part of the land was deemed too dangerous to inhabit, some became a wildlife refuge, and other parcels, despite the misgivings of environmentalists, welcomed real estate developers.

Other Economic Drivers

As significant as defense and aerospace were to the metropolitan area's well-being after World War II, other engines also powered the economy. By merging with Miller and Molson, Coors Brewing kept afloat in the turbulent international suds market. When the Gates family sold Gates

Rubber to Tompkins, a British firm, in 1996, they walked away with more than a billion dollars. But Tompkins did not walk away from the Mile High City, where it kept more than a thousand employees at Gates headquarters. Extractive industries continued to be mainstays, with petroleum companies creating a raft of local millionaires and at least one multibillionaire—Philip Anschutz. Since the early 1860s, Denver had also been an important regional banking center. By the 1990s, its venerable old banks, such as First National and Colorado National, had been absorbed by out-of-state behemoths such as Wells Fargo and US Bank, which competed for deposits with investment companies such as Janus Capital Group, headquartered in Denver. Other ventures were new. In the 1950s, Bill Daniels began building his cable empire, which made the Denver area a hub for other cable and antennae TV providers, including billionaires John Malone, whose complex conglomerate reached across the United States and into Europe, and Charles Ergen, who in 1980 cofounded what became DISH Network.

Unlike many cities in the East and Midwest where factories, unable to match foreign competition, rusted away, Denver, which had not developed much heavy industry, usually enjoyed good times, punctuated by occasional downturns, as in the early 1980s because of a crash in oil prices, in the early 1990s because of the collapse of some local savings-and-loan associations, and in 2008 as part of the national Great Recession. Normally, however, the trend line slanted up, as the city and its suburbs added to the economic base by attracting regional, national, and some international headquarters of firms whose executives and employees appreciated the region's climate, year-round recreational opportunities, good hospitals, sports and cultural attractions, and youthful vibrancy.

New Leadership: Palmer Hoyt and Quigg Newton

In 1946 journalist John Gunther in his book *Inside USA* portrayed Denver as a stagnant place dominated by its wealthy families. His snapshot was correct, but he did not sense how quickly the picture was going to change. An inkling of that transformation came early in 1946 when the *Denver Post,* a newspaper with immense local influence, put William Shepherd, its longtime editor, out to pasture. In his stead, Helen Bonfils, who controlled the *Post*, installed Palmer Hoyt, formerly editor of the *Portland Oregonian*. Hoyt reveled in Chamber of Commerce booster-ism but also understood there was a wider world, and he sported a pro-gressive streak uncommon among the city's old guard and much of its citizenry. By putting Bill Hosokowa, a Japanese American, and George Brown, an African American, on the *Post*'s staff, Hoyt signaled that the paper was breaking from its narrow-minded, xenophobic past.

Hoyt obviously wanted change, and as part of that agenda he was open to replacing Benjamin F. Stapleton as mayor. "Interminable Ben," as *Time* dubbed him, began his political career in Robert Speer's era. He won the mayor's chair in 1923 and with one four-year gap (1931–35) con-tinued to sit in it until 1947. Hoyt's task was made easy because waiting in the political wings was an energetic man half Stapleton's age, a Yale graduate, a navy veteran, a member of a respected and wealthy local family, but attuned to bringing Denver out of its shell. His only political liability seemed to be his name. Although his first name was James, he went by his middle name, Quigg. That allowed people to joke that he was a cookie, a Fig Newton. Supported by both the *Post* and the city's other major paper, the *Rocky Mountain News*, Newton trounced Stapleton.

During Newton's eight years as mayor, the city saw more govern-mental reform than it had during Stapleton's decades and more civic progress than it had since the 1920s. He initiated civil service job pro-tection for city employees, who previously had been political appointees expected to vote for the incumbent mayor. He pushed citizens to expand the airport, to build a new central library, to create an effective planning commission, to clean up rat-infested alleys, to improve the antiquated traffic system, to upgrade Denver General Hospital, to pay city workers decent wages, and to rethink their attitudes toward minority groups. He was, as has been typical of many US mayors, responsive to the needs and wishes of business interests, but unlike many local politicians of the 1930s and 1940s, he was willing to ask for tax increases to modernize the city.

From a twenty-first-century vantage point, Denverites might wish Newton had done some things differently. Had he foreseen the growth of air traffic, the impact of jet noise, the spread of Denver, and the rise of Aurora, he might have relocated Stapleton Airport rather than expand-ing it near residential areas—a misstep that cost billions of dollars to

James Quigg Newton modernized Denver during his 1947–55 mayorship, transforming a sleepy streetcar town into an up-to-date city with greatly improved health care, better libraries, and a jet-friendly airport. Courtesy Denver Public Library.

correct when the city relocated the airport. Had he foreseen the rapidity and magnitude of suburban population growth, he might have annexed more land, thereby broadening the city's tax base and giving planners a chance to impose some order on what became vast sprawl.

Had Newton delved into the inner workings of the police department, he might have detected barrels of rot. Sadly, police corruption got little attention until 1960, when, during the administration of Mayor Richard Batterton, exposés published in the *Rocky Mountain News* embarrassed Denverites by revealing that some cops were robbers and that other cops were covering up for them. The state of Colorado stepped in to clean up the police department, and eventually more than fifty policemen were indicted and many of them sent to jail. But to fault Newton because he could not see the future would be wrong. His foresight was flawed, as is everyone's, yet he was still one of the city's best mayors.

New Downtown

In 1946 the central business district reflected nearly two decades of stagnation. Few significant buildings rose during the Great Depression or World War II years. Shots of the skyline in the mid-1940s show the slender Daniels and Fisher tower, a 330-foot structure at Sixteenth and Arapahoe Streets, as the city's tallest building, just as it had been on its completion in 1911. Six decades later the picture had changed dramatically. The transformation began in the 1950s with the construction of such buildings as architect I. M. Pei's Mile High Center at Seventeenth Street and Broadway—remarkable for its sleek modernity, which stood in soaring contrast to many ponderous stone and brick structures, earthbound reminders of the past. The modernization continued in the late 1950s with the Hilton Hotel and adjoining May-D&F department store at Sixteenth Street and Tremont Place, which featured another relatively small Pei gem—a hyperbolic paraboloid that the city failed to save from demolition in 1996. The completion of the forty-two-story Brooks Tower, an apartment building at Fifteenth and Arapahoe Streets, in the late 1960s gave hope to those who feared that downtown risked becoming a place populated in the day only.

Suburban growth, shopping malls both in Denver and in the suburbs, and the decline of downtown theaters and department stores all increasingly threatened the health of the central business district by the late 1950s. Many of its buildings dated to the 1879–92 boom, and landownership was fragmented, making it difficult to assemble sites suitable for skyscrapers. Developer George M. Wallace capitalized on the demand for up-to-date office space by abandoning the core city. With eighty thousand dollars in borrowed money, he bought 40 acres of farmland fifteen miles southwest of downtown, where he created the Denver Technological Center, a complex with modern buildings and ample parking, which opened in 1962 and grew by 1980 to more than 800 acres. When Hewlett-Packard decided to build in the Denver area, it located its plant, which opened in 1962, not in Denver but in Longmont.

Skyline and Auraria Urban Renewal Projects

Decentralization threatened the central business district. As was the case in many US cities, downtown boosters looked to urban renewal as a way to revitalize the center. The Skyline Urban Renewal Project of the late 1960s cleared 113 acres of downtown buildings to make large tracts suitable for behemoth high-rises. To soften the impact of those hulks, planners commissioned noted landscape designer Lawrence Halprin to craft Skyline Park, a three-block shady oasis of trees, grass, recessed seating areas, and waterfalls between Fifteenth and Eighteenth Streets along

Arapahoe Street. Skyline fell victim to commercial pressure in the early twenty-first century, leading to the leveling of its canyons and the destruction of many of its trees.

Another demolition derby in the early 1970s saw bulldozers smashing homes and commercial buildings on the southwest fringe of downtown to clear 169 acres for the Auraria Higher Education Center, so named because it occupied much of the site of the 1858–60 gold-rush town of Auraria. Displaced Hispanic residents complained but lacked the money and the clout to resist renewal enthusiasts. Beginning in the mid-1970s, a campus sprouted that by 2016 served some forty-three thousand students enrolled at Metropolitan State University of Denver, the University of Colorado–Denver, and the Community College of Denver. Initially a well-planned facility with consistent architecture, cost-effective use of space, and openness to the city, Auraria lost its openness in the early twenty-first century when it walled much of itself off from downtown by throwing up grandiose perimeter buildings.

The city's three tallest buildings, all around seven hundred feet, the fifty-two-story, cash-register-shaped United Bank Center (later Wells Fargo), the fifty-three-story 1801 California, and the boxy fifty-six-story Republic Plaza, erupted in the early to mid-1980s largely because of the 1970s oil boom. The 1990s saw the residential flowering of the Golden Triangle, land to the southeast of downtown, and the rise of Lower Downtown (dubbed LoDo), which prospered after the 1988 designation of the LoDo Historic District, the 1995 building of Coors Field, and the 2015 remake of Union Station as a hotel and shopping mall. Redevelopment of the South Platte River Valley west of Union Station made derelict land suitable for high-rises and riverside parks and provided a segue into residential development in nearby North Denver. In the 1990s and early in the 2000s, similar activity east and northeast of downtown made parts of those areas into densely populated apartment neighborhoods that melded into venerable historic districts, such as Curtis Park.

Department stores, particularly after the 1970s, abandoned the central business district to relocate in shopping malls scattered throughout the metropolitan area. One of the earliest, Merchants Park on South Broadway and West Exposition Avenue opened in 1951 but was too small to seriously threaten downtown. A much larger ongoing threat

Ninth Street Historic Park, a block of vintage homes complete with corner grocery, has been restored as the heart of the Auraria Higher Education Center, Colorado's most popular campus, with some forty-three thousand students, shared by the Community College of Denver, Metropolitan State University of Denver, and the University of Colorado–Denver. Photo by Tom Noel.

The Navarre, one of downtown's oldest landmarks, has been restored as the American Museum of Western Art. Photo by Roger Whitacre, courtesy Denver Public Library.

came from architect Temple Buell's Cherry Creek Shopping Center at First Avenue and University Boulevard. It opened in 1953 on forty-nine acres, scarcely three miles southeast of downtown, on a site Buell had purchased in 1925 for twenty-five thousand dollars. Redeveloped and expanded, its upscale stores continued attracting shoppers from near and far into the twenty-first century.

By 1965 there were more than fifty shopping centers in the metropolitan area, and downtown department stores were withering. As they died, the core city remained alive in part because of the Sixteenth Street Mall, another I. M. Pei creation, which, beginning in the early 1980s, gave the central city a human-scale main street, more welcoming to pedestrians than skyscraper-lined canyons. Department stores, such as the Denver Dry Goods Company; banks, such as Colorado National; warehouses; and other buildings were reincarnated as lofts, apartments, and hotels. Larimer Square (a historic preservation triumph spearheaded in the mid-1960s by developer Dana Crawford), the Denver Pavilions, the Tabor Center, new hotels and restaurants, residential towers, brewpubs and nightclubs, and the Santa Fe and other arts districts similarly drew people from the periphery into the center.

Core City Attractions

Museums and other attractions also contributed to the core's vibrancy. Among the most significant were the Denver Performing Arts Complex, the Denver Public Library, the Denver Art Museum (DAM), the History Colorado Center, the Clyfford Still Museum, the Kirkland Museum of Fine and Decorative Arts, the Museum of Contemporary Art, the American Museum of Western Art housing the Anschutz Collection, the US Mint, the state capitol, the Children's Museum of Denver, Elitch Gardens Theme Park, Coors Field, the Pepsi Center, and the Denver Broncos Sports Authority Field at Mile High. A few miles east of downtown, the Denver Zoo, the Denver Museum of Nature and Science, and the Denver Botanic Gardens added to the city's vitality.

DAM grew out of the Artists' Club, a group founded in the 1890s. In 1949 the museum secured an ideally located permanent downtown home by remodeling old buildings between Acoma and Bannock Streets on

West Fourteenth Avenue, steps away from the City and County Building. Over the years, it received splendid gifts, including Anne Evans's collection of Native American and Hispanic art. Evans, one of the city's great cultural leaders, appreciated Indians more than her father, territorial governor John Evans, did. In the late 1960s, local architect James Sudler teamed with Italian architect Gio Ponti to create the fortresslike, tile-clad Ponti-Sudler building at West Fourteenth Avenue and Bannock Street. In 2006 the titanium-sheathed, angle-worshipping Hamilton wing designed by Daniel Libeskind was crowded onto a nearby site at West Thirteenth Avenue and Acoma Street.

DAM's wings juxtaposed with the Denver Public Library, the north section (1956) designed by Burnham Hoyt and the south (1995) by Michael Graves, created architectural exuberance dangerous to the sensibilities of the overly sensitive. More restrained attractions nearby include the Byers-Evans House Museum (1883–89) at 1310 Bannock. Once the home of pioneer newspaper editor William N. Byers, it later belonged to territorial governor John Evans's son William Gray Evans and his descendants. To the south, the Clyfford Still Museum (2011, architect Brad Cloepfil) at 1250 Bannock houses a large collection of Still's works. And a short walk to the southeast, history fans enjoy the History Colorado Center (2009) on East Twelfth Avenue and Broadway, designed by David Tryba.

Like the art museum, the zoo, today creatively crowded into eighty acres in the northeast quadrant of City Park, evolved slowly from its inception as a miserable collection of caged animals in the mid-1890s. "Cookie," its first elephant, did not arrive until 1950, and not until the mid-1970s did its exotic birds get a good home. In the late 1980s, it added Northern Shores, allowing visitors to go paw to paw with polar bears. Predator Ridge (2004) created an expansive savanna-like, rock-ledged habitat for African hyenas, wild dogs, crowned cranes, banded mongooses, and room for two prides of lions to prowl, preen, and pose. Wolf Pack Woods (1988) has been a howling success but was topped by the Toyota Elephant Passage (2012), featuring two miles of interconnected trails on ten acres of varied terrain in one of the largest and most complex elephant habitats in North America. While adding new exhibits and species, the zoo has maintained its grand old National Register attraction, Bear Mountain, a national pioneer in moving animals out of cages and into expansive natural environments.

The zoo's near neighbor in City Park, the Denver Museum of Nature and Science, opened in 1908 with a collection of Colorado plants and animals assembled by naturalist Edwin Carter. In the late 1920s, its director, Jesse D. Figgins, won national attention when his excavations near Folsom, New Mexico, demonstrated that people had been in North America for thousands of years. With impressive fossil displays, a superb mineral collection, special exhibits, a planetarium, an IMAX theater, and life-size wildlife dioramas, the museum ranks among the nation's best nature and science venues. Like many cultural attractions, it has benefited from the donations of wealthy individuals and foundations and has paid tribute to its donors by naming things for, among others, Anschutz, Boettcher, Coors, Gates, Leprino, and Phipps.

The Denver Botanic Gardens remained a stepchild among the city's attractions until it moved in the late 1950s from City Park to twenty-three acres near East Tenth Avenue and York Street, where Mount Calvary Catholic Cemetery had been. Backed by a gift from the Boettcher Foundation, architects Victor Hornbein and Edward White designed a stunning conservatory that opened in 1966. In 2009 the Gardens added a parking garage with a rooftop children's garden. An outdoor dining garden and the Science Pavilion were among many other improvements. Unable to significantly expand at their York Street site, the Gardens overflowed to a large tract on the south side of Chatfield Reservoir in Jefferson County, where visitors can see a five-acre working farm with vintage structures, a corn maze, a nature trail, and a seventy-acre nature preserve along Deer Creek.

Challenges

From the vantage point of the early twenty-first century, most observers would likely have agreed that Denver had avoided the central-city decay that afflicted many other cities. Challenges, however, remained. Drought years let citizens know that they did not have enough water—especially if they wanted to cultivate tens of thousands of acres of green lawns in a region that was at best semiarid. Traffic gridlock let drivers know that without improved highways and public transportation, they would increasingly languish in frustratingly slow traffic. Meeting those and other challenges, ranging from bad air to an outdated airport, became increasingly difficult, as the city of Denver lost much of its clout as its proportion of the metropolitan area's population declined. In 1950 more than 70 percent of the area's population lived within Denver's city limits; by 2010 more than 75 percent of the area's population lived outside Denver's city limits.

Many factors contributed to that shift. When it was established in 1902, the City and County of Denver (the boundaries of the city and the county are the same) constituted about fifty-nine square miles. Between 1902 and 1940, when it would have been fairly easy to expand into sparsely populated unincorporated tracts, particularly in Jefferson and Arapahoe Counties, there was enough vacant land within Denver to accommodate much of its population growth, so there was no pressure to annex.

Beginning in 1940, the city awoke from its torpor and began adding land, although sometimes city fathers hesitated to expand because the city would need to provide costly services. In the 1960s and early 1970s, as Denver increasingly recognized that it needed land to grow, it added more than forty square miles, mainly to the southwest, southeast, and northeast of its previous limits. Those annexations angered many suburbanites, who valued their independence and often regarded Denver as an overbearing land grabber. By incorporating previously unincorporated areas and establishing new towns such as Lakewood, which combined various Jefferson County entities, suburban residents blocked Denver.

Finally, the provisions of the 1974 Poundstone Amendment to the Colorado Constitution destroyed Denver's ability to annex unless it could get county commissioners from affected areas to agree. An arrangement in 1988 with Adams County allowed Denver to annex fifty-four square miles for a new airport, but that fiefdom came with restrictions. Some suburbs such as Englewood found it difficult to add acreage because they were blocked by other incorporated places such as Littleton. In other instances, better-situated cities such as Aurora, Arvada, and Westminster expanded like spilled syrup.

Solving regional problems that transcended political jurisdictions required cooperation that was often difficult and sometimes impossible to achieve among competing cities and towns. By 1970, when the US Census revealed that more metro-area people lived outside the city of Denver than within it, Denver's story was at least as much about the suburbs as it was about the core.

Chapter Eleven

Suburbanization

By 2010 more than three-quarters of all metro-area residents lived outside Denver's city limits in a mushrooming ring of suburban cities and towns. These included Aurora, the state's third-largest city after Denver and Colorado Springs; Lakewood, the fifth largest; Thornton, the sixth; and Westminster, the seventh. Suburban growth sprang from many sources. The robust post–World War II Colorado economy, the climate, and nearby mountains attracted people to the Front Range. Denver's failure to annex aggressively in the early 1950s prompted suburban development. In the 1960s and beyond, suburbs' resistance to Denver annexations slowed the city's territorial growth and gave scope to suburban expansion.

School busing in Denver aimed at achieving integrated schools played a role in suburban growth by causing some whites to flee and by making the core city less attractive to some newcomers. Between 1970 and 1990, Denver's population declined by more than 45,000. Yet even had there been no busing, Denver's room for expansion was limited. In the Denver area, unlike in many other metropolises, the suburban explosion was fueled less by people moving away from the core than by new arrivals who found homes with two-car garages, three and four bedrooms, and two or more bathrooms at affordable prices in the suburbs. High-tech and aerospace facilities' appetites for large plots of land also benefited communities on the urban periphery. Nevertheless, after 1990 Denver resumed its growth, adding more than 130,000 people in twenty years, which made it in 2010 still the most populous city and the most populous county in a megalopolis of more than 3 million people.

2010 US Census Populations	
Adams County	441,603
Arapahoe County	572,003
Boulder County	294,567
Broomfield City and County	55,889
Denver City and County	600,158
Douglas County	285,465
Jefferson County	534,543

Broomfield City and County

A suburban boom northwest of Denver fostered the creation of Broomfield, which became Colorado's sixty-fourth county on November 15, 2001, taking bits of territory from Adams, Boulder, Jefferson, and Weld Counties to make it 33.6 square miles. Named for the broom corn once raised there, Broomfield's agricultural roots generated the town's first two high-rises—the Zang and Coors grain elevators along the Union Pacific tracks. Church's Station, as Broomfield was first called, after a pioneer ranching family, caught the attention of Adolph Zang, a Denver beer baron. In 1879 he bought four thousand acres, where he raised French Percheron horses, fruit trees, and berries on his Elmwood Stock Farm. Church's Station became a town after the 1881 arrival of the Union Pacific Railroad. Around the UP depot, now the Broomfield Museum at 2201 West 110th Avenue, the community sprang up. It remained a rural hamlet for seventy years, not passing the 100-resident mark until 1950.

The 1952 opening of the Denver-Boulder Turnpike accelerated Broomfield's transition from ranches to ranch houses. In 1955 the Turnpike Land Company bought a large chunk of the Zang spread and built the Broomfield Heights residential subdivision, complete with a shopping center. Today, Interlocken Office Park, residential subdivisions, the vast Flatiron Crossing Mall, and a major events center make it likely that Broomfield will soon grow to 100,000 people.

Douglas County

Douglas County, a rural place with fewer than 9,000 people as late as 1970, emerged as one of the fastest-growing counties in the United States during the 1990s and 2000s. Castle Rock, the county seat, boomed with residential subdivisions and a factory outlet complex and became one of the wealthiest and most politically conservative of Denver's suburbs. Park Meadows, the state's largest shopping mall, typified the transformation of Highlands Ranch, on the northern edge of the county. That twenty-three-square-mile Hereford haven, bought by California developer Mission Viejo in 1978, grew into an unincorporated community of more than 100,000, displacing Castle Rock as the county's largest town. Lack of water seemed to be the only impediment to Douglas County growth, forcing developers to dig deeper into the Denver Aquifer or buy water rights from agricultural users.

To prevent the I-25 corridor from turning into a strip city from Highlands Ranch to Colorado Springs, a coalition, including cable telecommunications magnate John Malone, the Nature Conservancy, the Trust for Public Lands, Douglas County, the State Historical Fund, and others, in 2000 bought the twenty-one-thousand-acre Greenland Ranch, the domain of the Higby family from 1909 until they sold it to developers in 1981. Saved from being carpeted by houses and strip malls, the spectacular spread south of Larkspur became open space, with an interpretive center and nature trail that opened

Greenland Ranch, saved in 2000 as open space, provides a rural escape along the heavily urbanized and suburbanized I-25 corridor between Denver and Colorado Springs. Photo by Tom Noel.

in 2003. Nevertheless, Douglas County's growth continued, with consequent increased traffic congestion along I-25. Allergic to taxes, the county, although the wealthiest per capita in the metro area, chose not to become part of the Regional Transportation District's sales tax district. Later, two towns on its northern edge, Lone Tree and Highlands Ranch, opted to allow RTD taxes so they could secure FasTracks light-rail connections.

Arvada

Arvada, eight miles northwest of central Denver, can claim the earliest well-documented gold discovery in the metropolitan area, which took place in 1850 on Ralston Creek, where California-bound prospectors panned some gold dust and named the creek after a member of their group. Twenty years later, Benjamin Franklin Wadsworth, namesake of Wadsworth Boulevard, founded the town, naming it after his wife's brother-in-law, Hiram Arvada Haskin. Before 1940 it was noted for its flour mill, goats, and Annual Harvest Festival. To ensure its future as a pleasant, orderly place, it hired Colorado's foremost landscape architect and civic planner, Saco R. DeBoer, in 1919 to design parks and plan development. To enhance its parks, it established a recreation district in 1955 that has sprinkled the city with playgrounds, three recreation centers, five swimming pools, an ice arena, forty tennis courts, a bowling alley, and a golf course. Along with 140 parks, Arvada boasts 125 miles of hiking, biking, and horseback trails. The Arvada Center for the Arts and Humanities and a lively "Olde Towne" city center give character to the once quiet backwater, which grew from 1,500 people in 1940 to become Colorado's eighth-largest city in 2010 with a population of more than 106,000.

Aurora

Aurora originated in 1891 with the founding of Fletcher, named for entrepreneur Donald K. Fletcher, who, broken by the panic of 1893, fled Colorado. In 1907 citizens, saddled with debts for a failed Fletcher water project, renamed the town Aurora, after the Roman goddess of the dawn portrayed in antiquity as rising out of the eastern sea with rosy fingers dripping dew. Today the goddess scatters her dew on the lawns of tens of thousands of tree-shaded homes, seas of cars, and oceans of asphalt. Explosive growth and an aggressive annexation policy have transformed the town of 3,437 in 1940 into Colorado's third-largest city with a 2010 population of 325,078. With more than 154 square miles, Aurora boasts more land than Denver, and because much of its acreage awaits development, Aurora will get larger.

Contributors to Aurora's success include Denver International Airport (DIA), which, although within Denver's city limits, is geographically more a part of Aurora than of Denver; Buckley Air Force Base; and the multihospital Anschutz Medical Campus. Established in the early 1940s as an offshoot of Lowry Army Air Force Base, which straddled the Denver-Aurora border, Buckley grew by the early twenty-first century into a mighty military complex, housing contingents from the US Army, Navy, Air Force, Coast Guard, and Marines as well as the Colorado Air National Guard. Although some flew F-16 jets and Apache helicopters, many of Buckley's warriors, such as the Coast Guard Cryptographical Unit, engaged in cerebral gymnastics, as they analyzed data gathered from satellites that monitored missile launches and other data so secret that perhaps even WikiLeaks will never know about it. Despite the mystery shrouding many Buckley operations, the base itself became increasingly visible in the 1970s because of giant white radomes, resembling Alaska-size golf balls, that shielded massive radar antennae from rain, snow, hail, and prying eyes. A few miles northwest of Buckley, the University of Colorado (CU) Health Sciences Center and Hospitals acquired the Fitzsimons Army Hospital site, which the army had abandoned. The emergence of CU's Anschutz Medical Campus gave Aurora the largest medical training and treatment center in the Rockies and helped attract Denver's Children's and Veterans' Hospitals to the Fitzsimons property.

Aurora, which touts itself as the "Gateway to the Rockies," takes pride in its accomplishments. Billboard regulations and building-height limitations ensure that its residents can usually see the Rockies. The Martin Luther King Jr. Library on Elmira Street and public art, including Lawrence Argent's illuminated streetcar in the median planter, brighten the old East Colfax Avenue strip where Aurora began, as does the nearby Galena Street Historic District of pioneer residences. The city offers more than ten parks, six thousand acres of open space, and Aurora

Reservoir, with a sandy beach, swimming, nonmotorized boating, fishing, hiking, and wildlife watching. Its eleven-hundred-acre Plains Conservation Center includes a reconstructed hamlet with a one-room school, a sod house, barn, chicken coop, blacksmith workshop, turkeys, and cows. The center also operates a seventy-eight-hundred-acre site on West Bijou Creek with creatures galore, even a buffalo herd, a reminder of the immense herds that once roamed the prairie upon which Aurora has sprung.

Although pre–World War II Aurora had been a small, cohesive community with a recognizable town center around East Colfax Avenue and Havana Street, it was so overwhelmed by growth in the 1950–80 period that it risked becoming little more than a loose collection of subdivisions. Bit by bit, it fashioned, as did many other suburbs, a sense of identity. To define its center, it named one of its parks City Center Park. Nearby, in a monumental centering effort, it grouped many of its government buildings, including the Municipal Center, which opened in early 2003; police department headquarters; the Central Library; a history museum; and the City Municipal Court, crowned by a sixty-five-foot

Aurora's Plains Conservation Center preserves a cluster of sod buildings and a patch of prairie where the deer and the antelope still play. Photo by Tom Noel.

dome with east windows to catch morning rays from the goddess of the dawn. Plans announced late in 2014 envisioned a memorial garden at the Municipal Center to remember the victims of the mass shooting at the nearby Century Aurora 16 Theater, where a dozen people were killed and seventy injured on July 20, 2012, a tragedy that gave Aurora national attention it did not want.

Many deserved credit for Aurora's success. In the 1960s, councilman Paul Beck and others convinced taxpayers to borrow millions to develop their own water supply, thereby gaining independence from the Denver Water Board. By 1967 Aurora, thanks to collaboration with Colorado Springs, was drawing water from Homestake Reservoir, on the western side of the Continental Divide, and subsequently it built a powerful water empire. Capable city managers and energetic mayors, including Norma Walker (mayor from 1965 to 1967 and the first woman to lead a large Colorado city) and Dennis Champine, pushed the city forward, despite occasional setbacks, such as the economic bust of the early 1980s. When Paul Tauer left the mayor's job after sixteen years in 2003, he was praised by Aurora partisans for snatching the University of Colorado's Heath Sciences Center away from Denver, for spearheading development of the city center area, and for pushing the building of tollway E-470, which propelled development on the eastern side of a city that, lured by the dawn goddess, seemed intent on spreading farther and farther east. His son, Ed Tauer, succeeded Paul and served as mayor until 2011, giving the city twenty-four years of Tauer leadership.

Boulder

Boulder became a significant town with a respectable business district and a strong sense of identity before being gradually and reluctantly engulfed in the metropolitan area, largely because US Highway 36 funneled development toward it. Demographers now include Boulder and its hinterland, a region with nearly 300,000 people, as part of the Denver-Aurora Combined Statistical Area. Deadwood Diggings, as Boulder was called before formation of the Boulder City Town Company, became Colorado's eleventh-largest city, with 97,385 people within its city limits in 2010. Shunning such status, it has struggled to keep its population under 100,000 and has led the state in restricting growth by creating greenbelts and limiting building permits.

Gold strikes first attracted settlers to Boulder; coal, tungsten, and oil later became more important. The University of Colorado, the city's main economic driver, enrolled 44 students and offered its first classes in 1877. After World War II, it developed first-rate science and engineering programs that attracted major federal scientific centers, such as the National Center for Atmospheric Research and the National Bureau of Standards, as well as such high-tech enterprises as IBM.

Frederick Law Olmsted Jr., America's leading landscape architect, gave Boulder a dream to which it has clung with his 1910 plan entitled "The Improvement of Boulder, Colorado": "The main lookout of citizens is not how to make money as quickly as possible so as to go somewhere else to enjoy life, but how to get as much satisfaction out of life as they can in a very agreeable locality." Boulder became a model of growth management in 1967 when residents voted for a sales tax to buy open space. That helped it save its mountain backdrop from development and gave it a buffer of farmland to the east. The town limited motor vehicle noise to eighty decibels, building heights to 55 feet, and new housing permits to a 2 percent annual increase. By protecting its spectacular setting, preserving its older neighborhoods, and restoring its main street as the Pearl Street Mall, it has cushioned residents against the shock of rapid growth.

Ironically, the town renowned for planning originated in a plan gone awry. Its founder, Captain Thomas A. Aikins, and ten other gold seekers hoped to reach the Cherry Creek diggings in 1858 but wound up instead at Boulder Creek, which Aikins named for its many boulders. Aikins and others founded "Boulder City" on February 10, 1859. They platted a two-mile-long town in the mouth of Boulder Canyon, offering four thousand home sites at one thousand dollars each. The lots, measuring 50-by-140-feet, were larger than the 25-by-125-foot parcels standard in Denver and elsewhere. The community's early interest in elbow room was reflected in the initial town plat's generous assignment of almost half the land to roads, alleys, parks, and public space.

Centennial

Centennial, a city southwest of Greenwood Village and south of Cherry Creek Reservoir, bested Boulder by about three thousand people to be Colorado's tenth-largest city in 2010. Unlike Boulder, it has a short past, having been incorporated in 2001 because Arapahoe County residents feared that nearby Greenwood Village would gobble up the area's sales-tax dollars. Promising to get along without much sales-tax revenue, Centennial faltered within a few years and raised taxes. Its motto, "Spirit of the Past," gladdens the heart of history buffs, but its past is shallower than that of many other suburbs. A better tag would be "Space Place," to honor one of its best-known businesses, United Launch Alliance, whose Atlas and Delta rockets propel defense satellites and space probes.

Commerce City

Until recently, Commerce City did not aspire to the trappings of more affluent suburbs. It welcomed even the smelliest agribusiness and industry, dating back to the hog farmers first settling along Sand Creek. They fed their pigs Denver's garbage and then sold the hogs back to Denver. Truck farmers also thrived along the South Platte River and its tributaries. To prevent annexation by Denver, residents of this part of southern Adams County incorporated as Commerce Town in 1952. After absorbing previously existing communities such as Adams City, Derby, Irondale, and Rose Hill, the town changed its name to Commerce City in 1962. Alfred Krough, a hog farmer, was elected the first mayor. When what is now Suncor, the state's only oil refinery, moved in, its fragrances competed with those of feedlots, hog farms, and slaughterhouses.

Between 2000 and 2010, Commerce City more than doubled its population, going from fewer than twenty-one thousand residents to nearly forty-six thousand. In the process, it risked losing its soul as a blue-collar industrial place noted for greyhound racing at Mile High Kennel Club (1949–2008). The 2007 opening of Dicks Sporting Goods Park, a $131 million stadium, home to the Colorado Rapids soccer team, near East Sixtieth Avenue and Quebec Street, put the town on the international soccer map; its Heritage and Cultural Center, dedicated in 2014, near East Sixtieth Avenue and Monaco Street; and its Buffalo Run Golf Course (1996), at West 112th Avenue and Chambers Road, showed that it intended to keep up with other suburbs. In 2007 some boosters, including newcomers in the Belle Creek and Reunion subdivisions northeast of old Commerce City, suggested jettisoning the town's heritage by renaming it. Most citizens, proud, as Carl Sandburg said of Chicago, to be "a tall bold slugger set vivid against the little soft cities," knocked out that idea at the polls.

Englewood

Sandwiched between Denver and Littleton, Englewood was Arapahoe County's largest city until Littleton boomed in the 1960s. Englewood's roots extend to Placer Camp, where the Russell party found gold in July 1858 and set up a short-lived camp at the confluence of Little Dry Creek and the South Platte River. Permanent settlement did not come until 1870, when Irishman Thomas Skerritt filed a 640-acre claim to what is now downtown Englewood. He supposedly locked the wheels on his wagon while driving back and forth to carve out South Broadway, the town's main street. Initially, the area suffered from a terrible reputation, partly because of the dog fights Skerritt staged at his ranch. Other sinners congregated in local taverns, prompting reformers to clean up and officially name the area Englewood in 1903. Clothed in virtue, it attracted the Lutheran-affiliated Swedish National Sanatorium for the Cure of Tuberculosis, which opened at West Hampden Avenue and Pearl Street in 1907. It has since evolved into the Swedish Medical Center, a full-service hospital with a retirement complex. Nearby Craig Hospital, another town mainstay since it moved to Englewood in the early 1970s, is nationally noted for rehabilitating spinal injuries.

In 1965 the town sold its City Park to the developers of Cinderella City, which claimed to be the largest shopping mall west of the Mississippi River. That now-gone shoppers paradise has been replaced by a new city center. Hoping to make up for selling its park, the town in recent years has expanded parks, built a recreation center, and turned Little Dry Creek and the South Platte River into landscaped foot and bicycle trails. In 2004 it made a big splash with its Pirates Cove water park. Locked in by Denver and Littleton as well as smaller, newer suburbs of

Bow Mar, Sheridan, and the two most affluent Denver suburbs, Cherry Hills and Greenwood Village, Englewood's population peaked at 33,965 in 1970 and has hovered around 30,000 ever since.

Golden

Thomas L. Golden, a prospector who settled in 1858 along Clear Creek where it emerges from the mountains to the plains, gave his name to the first town and county seat of Jefferson County. George West, a writer for the *Boston Transcript,* presided over the Boston Town Company, which invested in the site. West and company founded Golden City in June 1859 on the north bank of Clear Creek on what would become Golden's main street, Washington Avenue. Gold mines up Clear Creek Canyon ensured that Golden would thrive as the canyon's gateway. Between 1862 and 1867, it served as Colorado's territorial capital, although legislators and officials usually preferred to congregate in Denver. William A. H. Loveland gave legislators meeting space in his building at Twelfth Street and Washington Avenue, today the Old Capitol Grill, in 1865. They stayed only a day before decamping to Denver, which in 1867 wrestled the capital designation

Golden clings to its small-town friendliness, suggested by its Washington Avenue Welcome arch. Photo by Tom Noel.

away from Golden. As consolation, the village captured the Colorado School of Mines (1874), which remains a significant local employer, as does the Coors Brewing Company, founded by Adolph Coors in 1873 at the base of South Table Mountain.

Boosters promoted their town as a rail and smelting hub but lost much of that business to Denver. Golden stagnated, declining from 2,730 in 1880 to 2,425 in 1930. After World War II, it began to grow. In 1977 it won a major federal facility and employer when the National Renewable Energy Laboratories (NREL) opened on the sunny southeast slope of South Table Mountain. NREL, dedicated to promoting energy efficiency and renewable energy, employs more than 2,500, including full- and part-time workers, interns, and contractors. It showcases energy-efficient buildings, a visitors center, and a museum. Near the intersection of West Sixth Avenue and Johnson Road, the prominently situated Jefferson County Government Center, sometimes irreverently referred to as the Taj Mahal, is far-enough southeast of Golden's center that it does not overwhelm the town's charm. The building, which opened in 1993, may represent Golden's revenge for losing its capital status to Denver. With more than a half-million square feet, it is more than twice the size of the state capitol, and it has a spectacular dome, reflecting that of Thomas Jefferson's Monticello home. It outdoes the capitol by providing drive-through service for people paying their taxes. Despite the Judicial Center and NREL, Golden remained a small suburb of 18,867 in 2010, partly because many of its citizens preferred a small pleasant town to a big unpleasant one. Steep foothills to the west and unoccupied mesas to the east also frustrate sprawl.

Lakewood

Lakewood was platted in 1889 by William A. H. Loveland; his wife, Miranda; and Charles Welch as a thirteen-block country town strung out along West Colfax Avenue, just beyond Denver's western boundary. Since then it has become Colorado's fifth-largest city, with a 2010 population of 142,980. Epitomizing the antiurban sentiment of many suburbanites, Lakewoodites, leery of municipal government, refused to incorporate until 1969. They fancied ranch houses and spacious lawns, preferring to identify with the rural ideals of rugged independence and the mountains to the west rather than the monster metropolis of which they haltingly became part.

In 1941 the federal government, whose expenditures can often make or break a town, shaped Lakewood's future by buying the Downing-Hayden Ranch, stretching from West Sixth to West Alameda Avenues, between Kipling and Union Streets, to provide a site for the Denver Ordnance Plant, which was operated by the Remington Arms Company. The thirty-five-million-dollar ammunition factory was guarded by concrete watchtowers and fifteen miles of chain-link fence topped by barbed wire that did not keep out coyotes looking for the turkeys once raised on the poultry farms thereabouts. After World War II, it morphed into the Denver Federal Center, which became one of the largest concentrations of federal workers outside Washington, DC, with some thirty agencies employing more than 10,000 people.

Typical of many of the Denver suburbs that grew so fast between 1950 and 1990 they overwhelmed the town cores they once had, Lakewood lacked an anchor. In 2004 it partially solved the problem by recycling a failed shopping mall to fashion a hub of civic and commercial activity. The mall, Villa Italia, at Wadsworth Boulevard and West Alameda Avenue, was the successor to the most opulent of Denver's country estates, Belmar, owned by May Bonfils Stanton, inheritor of part of the fortune amassed by her father, Frederick, copublisher of the *Denver Post*. For decades, the regal May enjoyed her Carrara-marble mansion, where she slept in a bed previously owned by French queen Marie Antoinette, sat in a crested chair that had cushioned Queen Victoria, and listened to a piano once played by Frederic Chopin. After her death in 1962, her toys and home vanished to make room for residences, businesses, a park, and Villa Italia. In the 1990s, the once posh Villa skidded into near emptiness. Lakewood turned 1.4 million square feet of blonde-brick blight into a civic triumph by enticing Continuum Partners to create the Belmar district. On 104 acres Continuum mixed residences, retailers, restaurants, professional offices, theaters, and other amenities into a compact, walkable neighborhood, proving that dead malls can be reborn. With the Lakewood Cultural Center (which opened in 2000), Belmar Library, Lakewood Heritage Center, and Belmar Park all within a mile of the densely populated Belmar residential-commercial assemblage, Lakewood provided a few of its citizens the blessings of a compact neighborhood.

Littleton

Little's Town or Littleton originated with Richard Sullivan Little, a New England engineer who settled on a farm on the South Platte River, seven miles south of Denver, in 1860. He and his partners built the Rough and Ready Flour Mill in 1867, turning its grindstones with ditch water diverted from the river. By the 1890s, the Rough and Ready had expanded into a four-story, brick-and-stone landmark at Santa Fe Drive and West Bowles Avenue. Next to the mill, Little laid out the town named for him. Spurring growth, both the Santa Fe and the Denver and Rio Grande railroads built depots connecting Littleton to Denver and the rest of the state. Little was appointed the town's first postmaster in 1869 and elected the area's first representative to the territorial legislature. He promoted his village as a pleasant alternative to the big, bad city to the north. Living comfortably on the profits of his mill and land sales, he built a still-standing stone house at 5777 South Rapp Street, where he died in 1899.

When the City and County of Denver was carved out of Arapahoe County in 1902, Littleton became the county seat for the remaining part of Arapahoe County. It ventured into various agricultural activities besides flour milling. Once it called itself the "Beekeeping Capital of Colorado." After the Merry Canning and Pickling Company became the lead industry in 1891, some dubbed it "Pickle Town." Littleton also attracted a leading mining equipment company, George Leyner's Engineering Works. The Red Comet Fire Extinguisher Company suffered one of the town's worst fires in 1946. Ignoring wisecracks, Red Comet rebuilt and urged Littleton to establish a professional fire department, which it finally did in 1960.

In the mid-1950s aviation giant Glenn L. Martin began building Titan rockets in its Waterton Canyon facility, southwest of Littleton. At first those intercontinental ballistic missiles tipped with city-busting hydrogen bombs were buried in undergrown silos to use against the Soviet Union in case of nuclear war. Other Titans sent mid-1960s Project Gemini astronauts into orbit around the earth. The July 29, 1960,

Littleton Independent estimated that "34 per cent of the Littleton homes are headed up by a breadwinner in the Martin Company." For more than a half century, federal dollars rained upon Martin and its successor companies, whose rockets propelled probes to Mars and the space beyond Pluto. Littleton's population likewise skyrocketed, soaring to 41,737 in 2010.

Thornton

Colorado governor Dan Thornton and Hollywood actress Jane Russell presided at the 1953 grand opening of Thornton, north of Denver. The city's developer, Sam Hoffman, named his creation for the popular governor. He named curvaceous Russell Boulevard for the raven-haired, shapely movie star. Boxy brick homes originally selling for eight to eleven thousand dollars were quickly snapped up during the post–World War II population boom. By 1990 Thornton housed 60,000 people and stretched to its current boundaries, roughly 88th to 144th Avenues, between I-25 on the west and the South Platte River on the east. The Thornton Town Center Mall helped provide something of a nucleus for this sprawling suburb, which surrounds on three sides the smaller suburb of Northglenn. With a 2010 population of more than 120,000, it has become Colorado's sixth-largest city.

Westminster

Edgar Bowles homesteaded the area northwest of Denver in 1871 and built the big red-brick home at 3924 West 72nd Avenue that was restored in 1988 as the Westminster Historical Society Museum. He raised majestic stable horses, became a member of the first school board, promoted organization of the town's first church, and oversaw Westminster's incorporation as a town in 1911. To coax the Denver Interurban Rail Line to Westminster, he donated land for the depot.

Westminster borrowed its name from Westminster University, a Presbyterian school founded in 1892 atop the highest hill in Adams County. The "Princeton of the West" erected a magnificent red sandstone castle designed by noted New York architect Stanford White. The faltering university, prominently sited at West 88th Avenue and Lowell Boulevard, closed after World War I. Resurrected in the 1920s as Belleview

College, it served as a seminary for the Pillar of Fire church, whose leader Bishop Alma White pioneered radio evangelism.

The hamlet matured slowly between 1920 (235 people) and 1950 (1,686). Growth accelerated with the 1952 completion of the Denver-Boulder Turnpike. Westminster's new city hall, which opened on a hill near I-25 in 1988, gave the town visibility, with its 136-foot clock tower echoing the London landmark at Westminster Palace that houses a single bell—Big Ben. Westminster residents can brag that their tower, although slimmer and only half the height of its distant English cousin, has fourteen bells to toll the hours to a city of more than 106,000 people.

Wheat Ridge

Immediately to the west of Northwest Denver and south of Arvada, Wheat Ridge extends from Sheridan Boulevard to Youngfield Street, between West 26th and West 56th Avenues. Originally farmland, it partially retained its bucolic character by becoming home to Crown

Hill Cemetery, at West 29th Avenue and Wadsworth Boulevard, which opened in 1907 and built its Tower of Memories in the 1920s. The town made a sweet contribution to American civilization early in the twentieth century by being the birthplace of Bill Harmsen, who with his wife, Dorothy, founded the Jolly Rancher Candy Company. Besides becoming a major tourist attraction, Jolly Rancher grew into a huge hard-candy business that gave the Harmsens money to indulge their passion for art, most of it western, which they donated to the Denver Art Museum in 2002. Wheat Ridge's 2010 population of slightly more than 30,000 put it among Denver's smaller suburbs.

Metro Area in 2010

By 2010 the Denver metropolitan area, including Boulder and its satellite towns, boasted a population of nearly 3 million. Denver itself was the nation's twenty-sixth-largest city, and Aurora took fifty-sixth place. Some suburbs, such as Cherry Hills Village, where two US secretaries of state—Condoleezza Rice and Madeleine Albright—attended high school, ranked among the nation's wealthiest small towns. Some, such as Sheridan, were better known for their Fords than their Ferraris. Some, such as Northglenn, were much the same as their near neighbors. Others, such as Brighton and Fort Lupton, retained some of their century-old distinctiveness. Collectively, Denver and its suburbs were home to a varied collection of people: some born in Colorado, some recent arrivals from other states, some immigrants from Africa, Asia, Europe, and Latin America. Together, they made Greater Denver a complex and occasionally troubled place.

Chapter Twelve

All the People

*W*hat is the city but the people?," a quotation from Shakespeare's *Coriolanus,* incised into the Fourteenth Street facade of the Wellington E. Webb Municipal Office Building in downtown Denver, gives citizens on their way to pay their taxes an opportunity to consider a complex question: "Who are the people of Denver?"

The People Before 1950

The city's first census, taken in 1860, showed a population largely made up of white English-speaking males between the ages of fifteen and forty from midwestern and northeastern states, with most born in the United States. During the next fifty years, those patterns shifted, with the male-female and age distribution patterns gradually mirroring those of older places in the country. The city's ethnic flavor also changed, as its economic opportunities, reputation as a healthy place, railroad accessibility after 1870, and demand for cheap labor attracted more foreign born, mainly of European background. Denver did not harbor the hundreds of thousands of Irish, Germans, Poles, and Italians who crowded into large eastern and midwestern cities in the nineteenth and early twentieth centuries or the legions of Scandinavians who made homes in Minnesota. Nor did it become a beacon for African Americans moving from the South, as did Chicago and Detroit. Yet for more than a century and a half, Denver's population has reflected the complex racial and ethnic mix that has made the United States an ever-changing "from many one" collection of people.

The 1910 US Census gives a snapshot of the city's people as they were a century ago. Around 207,000 of its 213,381 citizens were counted as white, with the remainder being "Negro" (5,426), Japanese (585),

Chinese (227), and American Indian (71). By reporting the numbers of foreign-born whites and the number of second-generation residents whose parents were born outside the United States, the census showed the strength of ethnic communities. Germans led, with more than 16,000, followed by the Irish, with more than 10,000. Russians, a category that included Poles, numbered around 9,300. The English, including Scottish, Welch, and Cornish, boasted around 8,000, as did the Swedish. Nearly 5,000 Italians, more than 2,800 Austrians (split among various groups, such as Serbs and Croatians from the Austrian Hapsburg Empire), more than 1,400 Norwegians, and more than 1,000 Danes added to the mix, as did other smaller contingents, including French, Swiss, and Dutch. Other divisions made the picture even more complex. Germans included Lutherans, Roman Catholics, Methodists, and Jews. Most Irish were Roman Catholic; a relative few, such as Robert Morris, the city's mayor from 1881 to 1883, were Protestant. Some of the English were Episcopalians, including Dean Henry M. Hart, who made Saint John's

The Emmanuel-Sherith Chapel/Synagogue reflects the ethnic evolution of many Denver neighborhoods. Founded in 1877 as an Episcopal chapel, it became a synagogue for East European Jews after Episcopalians moved to Capitol Hill. This landmark is preserved at the Auraria Higher Education Center as a student art gallery. Photo by Tom Noel.

Cathedral a bastion of English culture; many others affiliated with Methodist or Presbyterian congregations. Polish migrants included Orthodox Jews and Roman Catholics.

Early twentieth-century Denver lacked the ghetto-like districts of foreign born found in large eastern and midwestern cities, but it had neighborhoods with high concentrations of particular groups. Many of its Irish, Germans (including German Jews), and Swedes lived in older areas near downtown. Poles and other Slavs built homes in Globeville and other smelter neighborhoods. Eastern European Jews congregated along West Colfax Avenue. Italians clustered northwest of the South Platte River, where some of them began their upward social ascent by raising vegetables. In the 1880s, the Chinese crowded into a few lower downtown locations, and in the early twentieth century much of the Japanese population lived in the vicinity of Nineteenth and Lawrence Streets. By 1910 the majority of African Americans had been packed into a few square miles centering on Five Points, an intersection of five streets at Twenty-Sixth Avenue and Welton Street. By custom and restrictive real estate covenants, the city kept some of its citizens—especially blacks, Chinese, Japanese, Italians, and Jews—residentially segregated. Sometimes symbols of prejudice, sometimes protective havens, ethnic neighborhoods, churches, and saloons gave newcomers an opportunity to cushion their adjustment to their new surroundings, as did the large Catholic school system, which kept many Irish, German, and Hispanic Catholics out of public schools.

The disparate groups usually tolerated each other, especially in good times, when jobs abounded. But sometimes economic competition and deep prejudices sparked clashes. Rioters opposed to the Chinese who worked for low wages tore up Chinese businesses and beat to death Lu Yang, a Chinese laundry worker, in late October 1880. In the mid-1890s the American Protective Association pressured the state to remove Catholics from state jobs. Anti-Semitic hooligans beat Jews Mendel Slatkin and Jacob Weisskind because they worked on Christmas. Weisskind died from his injuries in early 1906. Blacks, Catholics, and Jews suffered from Ku Klux Klan bigotry in the 1920s. When in 1921 Walter R. Chapman, an African American, bought a home at 2112 Gilpin Street, in a white neighborhood, someone bombed his house. He sold to another

African American, and the place was bombed a second time. Brave blacks who attempted to swim at the city-run beach on Smith's Lake in Washington Park in August 1932 were driven away by a stick-wielding, stone-throwing mob. Reflecting the attitudes of many Coloradans, Governor Edwin C. Johnson ordered a blockade along the state's southern border in April 1936 to keep out poor people—most of them Hispanic.

Turbulent Times, 1950s–1990s

By the early 1950s, the friction between the wider society and some of the immigrant groups of fifty years earlier, if not completely gone, was fading. The anti-Catholicism of the 1920s still smoldered but did not stop Thomas G. Currigan, an Irish Catholic, from becoming mayor in 1963. His successor, William H. McNichols Jr., mayor from 1968 to 1983, was also Irish and Catholic. Jews, though not welcome in some areas, enjoyed more freedom of settlement than fifty years earlier. Hilltop, for example, an upscale residential area between Eighth and Alameda Avenues, east of Colorado Boulevard and west of Holly Street, emerged in the 1940s and 1950s as a neighborhood open to Jews and their Temple Emanuel Synagogue.

Blacks

The placid veneer was deceptive. Beneath the surface lurked old racial attitudes and continuing injustices—employment, educational, housing, and recreational inequities among them—that fed anger and resentment, especially among blacks and Hispanics. The black population, which increased from 7,204 in 1930 (less than 3 percent of the total population) to 30,251 in 1960 (about 6 percent of the population), found most of the city off-limits when they wanted to buy homes, except in the Five Points district and areas to the east of Five Points, which in the 1940s and 1950s became increasingly African American. Most whites preferred to keep blacks out of sight. In September 1951, when George Brown, an African American reporter for the *Denver Post,* tried to swim at Lakeside Amusement Park's pool in North Denver, the manager warned him that other swimmers might throw rocks at him. When he visited the Crest-View Trailer Camp at 5545 Federal Boulevard, he was told, "We don't have restrictions on pets, but we have to draw the line on Negroes."

Rachel Noel knew much about segregation. Born in Virginia in 1918, she grew up unable to attend the same school as whites, to drink from the same drinking fountains, or use the same restrooms. In 1949 she and her husband, Edmond, a physician, moved to Denver, where he joined the staff of Rose Hospital, the only local hospital willing to hire a black medical doctor. Elected to the school board in 1965 as its first black member, she asked why the city's schools were segregated. Administrators claimed that some schools had heavy African American enrollments because the schools reflected neighborhood populations. Noel saw that as neighborhoods became increasingly black, bureaucrats rearranged school boundaries to block integration. To right that wrong, the school board in 1968 adopted the Noel Resolution, which envisioned busing students to achieve more racial balance. A year later, voters reacted by replacing probusing board members with antibusers, who scuttled Noel's program. Integrationists then filed a case, *Keyes v. School District No. 1*, in federal court. In a series of court rulings culminating in a 1973 US Supreme Court decision, judges ordered Denver to integrate its schools. That mandate, which also made clear that Hispanic students had a right to integrated education, led to federal court supervision of the schools and to considerable busing.

Many resisted busing. Some whites moved to the suburbs; others put their children in private schools. In February 1970, someone dynamited thirty-eight parked public school buses, destroying twenty-three of them. To prevent Denver's school district from expanding, Freda Poundstone, a lobbyist, crafted an amendment to the Colorado Constitution that made it extremely difficult for Denver to annex land. During the next quarter century, public school enrollment dropped, and many remaining students were either Hispanic or African American, so integration remained an elusive goal in 1995 when federal district judge Richard Matsch ended court supervision. By the early twenty-first century, the city's schools were only around 20 percent white.

Chicanos and the Crusade for Justice

Like Rachel Noel, Rodolfo "Corky" Gonzales, born in Denver in 1928, wanted change. His migrant-worker parents, as was the case with many Hispanics, toiled on farms spring through fall and spent winter months in

Denver. Pay was low, work seasonal, stability elusive. By the time Gonzales graduated from West High School, he had attended nine schools. For him, as for practically all poor—the vast majority were poor—Hispanic kids in the 1940s, there was no higher education except the college of hard knocks. An excellent boxer, Gonzales fought his way to national ranking as a featherweight. Later, as a reward for his work as a Democratic Party activist, he was made chairman of Denver's War on Poverty Program. Forced out of that faction-ridden agency, he abandoned traditional politics and in 1966 founded his own movement, the Crusade for Justice.

Spurred by Gonzales's charisma, the Crusade for Justice purchased an old church at Sixteenth Avenue and Downing Street for its headquarters. It published a cocky newspaper, *El Gallo,* and established a school, Escuela Tlatelolco. It celebrated Gonzales's poem "Yo Soy Joaquín" (I am Joaquin), which told of the long, complex, painful, and triumphant history of the people who became Chicanos. It proudly represented Chicanos, preferring that term of identity

During the 1970s, Chicanos marched in protest of the second-class citizenship for the first Euro-American group to explore, map, and settle Colorado. "We did not cross the border," some declared. "The border crossed us." Courtesy Denver Public Library.

because it stressed the mixed Hispano-Indian ancestry and the connection of many of its adherents to relatively recent migrants from Mexico. It attacked the police for alleged mistreatment of Chicano youth. It lambasted public schools for insensitivity to Chicano culture and for lagging in hiring and promoting Chicanos. It urged teenagers to get educated, to shun drugs, and to take pride in their heritage. Ernesto Vigil in his book *The Crusade for Justice: Chicano Militancy and the Government's War on Dissent* credits the Crusade for Justice with many virtues, including giving Chicano youth an alternative to gang membership.

Good works, however, did not impress many people, who fixated on the Crusade's confrontational rhetoric. A sign posted in a northwestern Denver park and reproduced in *El Gallo* in July 1973 made Chicano anger obvious and to many frightening:

> If blood is going to flow, then let
> It flow all over town. If gas is going
> To be used then let it be used all over
> Town. If pigs [police] are going to run wild
> Then let them run wild all over town. And if we're to be
> Disrupted and violated then let
> This whole . . . . town be
> Disrupted and violated.

Tensions occasionally boiled over, with the most serious confrontation occurring shortly after midnight on March 17, 1973, when police clashed with Chicanos attending a party at an apartment owned by the Crusade for Justice near its headquarters. By the time the shooting stopped, a twenty-year-old Chicano, Luís Martínez, lay dead; a dozen cops, including the wounded officer who shot Martínez, were hurt; and a portion of the second story of the apartment building had been blown up—perhaps by a police grenade or perhaps from explosives stored there. Crusade partisans saw the maelstrom as proof of police overkill and dubbed it the St. Patrick's Day Massacre. The police and others viewed it as evidence of radicals run amuck.

To the battles between the Crusade for Justice and the police was added internal strife that tore the Chicano-Hispanic community apart.

Historian Richard Gould in his book *The Life and Times of Richard Castro* recounts that when Castro, a young activist who did not support the Crusade, was shot by a Crusade partisan, *El Gallo* published a photo of the bleeding Castro with the warning, "If you can't do anything for the movement, don't do anything against it or it may cost you your life."

The fractures within the Chicano-Hispano community reflected in part the ancestry of the city's Latinos. Some were descendants of Coloradans, New Mexicans, and Texans, who had been in the Southwest for centuries. Other, more recent, arrivals were either from Mexico or the sons and daughters of Mexican nationals who had been drawn north, mainly after 1910, to work in the sugar beet fields of Colorado. Given those divisions and the friction between Chicanos and the wider society, it is amazing that within a decade of the St. Patrick's Day Massacre, Denver would elect its first Hispanic mayor. Partly, the growth of the Hispanic population explained the political shift. In 1960 federal census takers counted 43,147 "Spanish-Americans" in Denver, or about 9 percent of the total population. By 1980 the number stood at 91,937, around 19 percent of the population.

Politics, 1960s–2010s

Politically motivated after more than a decade of strife and mobilized by numerous activists besides Gonzales, Latinos by 1983 were ready to unite to help make Federico Peña mayor. Peña's chief opponents, district attorney Dale Tooley and incumbent mayor William H. McNichols Jr., carried baggage that hurt them. Tooley had been district attorney in the 1970s, a position that put him at odds with many Chicanos. McNichols's father, William, had been city auditor and his brother, Stephen, Colorado's governor. When Thomas G. Currigan resigned as mayor in 1967 because of the post's then paltry salary of fourteen thousand dollars a year, McNichols took over the job. He used his political machine to take the job again in 1971, 1975, and 1979, relying in part on antibusing Democrats and Republicans to keep him in office. Forward looking in some ways, he successfully persuaded voters to support taxes for civic improvements. His work to secure the Winter Olympics for Denver and mountain venues turned out less successfully. In 1972 Colorado taxpayers refused to

Federico Peña, Denver's first Latino mayor (1983–91), became one of the city's most energetic and accomplished leaders. Courtesy Tom Noel Collection.

Wellington E. Webb, Denver's first African American mayor (1991–2003), completed Denver International Airport in 1995, launched redevelopment of the Lowry and Stapleton neighborhoods, and doubled the city's park space. Courtesy VISIT DENVER.

fund infrastructure for the events, slated for 1976. This rare upset of the progrowth crowd fueled the expansion of a burgeoning environmental movement.

Energetic and charismatic, the thirty-six-year-old Peña adroitly portrayed McNichols and Tooley as worn-out politicians of yesteryear. Peña offered much. Born in Laredo, Texas, holding a law degree from the University of Texas, he came to Denver in 1973. In the late 1970s, he won a seat in the Colorado House of Representatives and quickly rose to be Democratic minority leader. Hispanics and Chicanos saw him as one of them. Some blacks, offended by McNichols's opposition to busing, preferred Peña. Some white Progressives trusted him as a peacemaker able to bridge ethnic chasms. Elements in the business community considered him a potential friend. In a June 1983 runoff election, Peña beat Tooley by forty-four hundred votes, and in 1987 Peña won an even narrower victory over attorney Don Bain to win a second term. Like McNichols, Peña persuaded voters to back bond issues for civic improvements. His biggest and most controversial project, Denver International Airport, a multibillion-dollar commitment on the city's part, was still unfinished when he left office in 1991. In 1993 he became US secretary of transportation in President Bill Clinton's cabinet.

Peña's successor, the city's first African American mayor, Wellington E. Webb, though Chicago-born, spent most of his life in Denver, where he won terms in the state legislature in the 1970s and the city auditor's post in 1987. A moderate like Peña, Webb weathered the 1970s without becoming enmeshed in the confrontational tactics favored by leaders such as Lauren Watson and his brother, Clarke, who with a coterie of Black Panthers frightened many whites. Mayor from 1991 to 2003, Webb, advised by his wife, Wilma, a political power in her own right, proved a friend to business, an advocate of city planning, a harmonizer of community interests, a library builder, an expander of city parks, and a man capable of getting the new airport operational.

As if to prove that the political pendulum had not swung totally in the direction of African American and Hispanic candidates, voters in 2003 elected brewpub owner and supercampaigner John W. Hickenlooper Jr. mayor. When Hickenlooper resigned in early 2011 to become Colorado's governor, Cuban-born Bill Vidal took the mayor's post for a few months until the election of Michael B. Hancock, the city's second African American mayor. A constant on the civic scene, city auditor Dennis Gallagher, a gregarious Irishman, entered his forty-fifth year in public office (state representative and senator, city councilman, city auditor) in 2015 as living proof that fighting for the people, challenging powers that be, quoting Shakespeare, and eating chicken at public functions could ensure political success.

Women

Women also fought for their rights. Among them Patricia S. Schroeder became a national star. Anti–Vietnam War activists in 1970 ended the career of Byron G. Rogers, the city's congressional representative since 1951. Taking advantage of a split Democratic Party, a Republican occupied Rogers's seat from 1971 to 1973. Schroeder patched up the Democratic Humpty Dumpty in 1972 to win election to the US House, from which she retired after twelve terms in 1997. A female rarity in Congress in her day, Schroeder, like Rogers, brought home federal dollars, and to the delight of Democrats and discomfort of Republicans, she, unlike Rogers, was full of wit. Her successor, Diana L. DeGette, continued the

Denver voters elected Patricia Scott Schroeder Colorado's first congresswoman in 1972. She proved to be the state's wittiest politician, with quips such as her retirement confession: "I have spent twenty-four years in a federal institution." Courtesy Tom Noel Collection.

Schroeder tradition in a lower key. Throughout the metropolitan area beginning in the 1970s, women increasingly won state legislature and city council posts. In 2014 Denver and Aurora's city councils both had more women than men, and the Lakewood council was evenly split. In 2015 more than 42 percent of the one-hundred-member Colorado General Assembly was composed of women, many from the metropolitan area.

The Lesbian, Gay, Bisexual, and Transgender (LGBT) Community

Up until the early 1970s, many Denverites regarded gay activity as "a crime against nature." During World War II, openly gay bars began popping up on Broadway. They became targets of the police department's vice squad, which entrapped patrons with propositions and then hauled them off to jail. Incensed by police tactics and prompted by gay activism in New York City and San Francisco, a handful of gays formed the Denver Gay Coalition in 1972. The following year, three hundred people showed up at a city council meeting, where activists persuaded the councilmen (there were then no women on the council) to rewrite four ordinances previously used to prosecute homosexuals. Two years later the city witnessed its first Gay Pride Parade, the harbinger of things to come, as gays developed a public voice that grew louder as the spread of AIDS in the 1980s caused many to emerge from closets of silence. They advocated for decent treatment of HIV and AIDS sufferers, and like blacks and Hispanics they fought against discrimination. Some, particularly in Denver and Boulder, lived openly gay lives, but many recognized that revealing their sexual orientation could mean ostracism and job loss. They found comfort in the late 1980s when Boulder forbade housing discrimination against gays and in 1991 when Denver did the same.

Such LGBT-friendly laws prompted conservative forces centered in Colorado Springs to push for Amendment 2, a November 1992 amendment to the Colorado Constitution forbidding cities and other political subdivisions from according protected status "based on homosexual, lesbian, or bisexual orientation." Voters approved the measure by nearly a 54-percent majority, which moved the LGBT community and their supporters to blast "the hate state" and to launch an economic boycott. The business community winced when gay-friendly groups began canceling conventions and vacations. Eventually, Colorado courts declared Amendment 2 unconstitutional, and in 1996 the US Supreme Court also struck it down.

The death of Amendment 2 did not end the bitter battles over the status of gays and lesbians. In the late 1990s, LGBT groups began pushing for recognition of same-sex marriages. Other Coloradans defended male-female unions, and in 2000 Governor Bill Owens signed a same-sex-marriage ban. Six years later, voters enshrined that prohibition in the state constitution. Annual efforts in the Colorado General Assembly to legalize same-sex civil unions were defeated until 2013, when the legislature finally permitted them. In 2014 a US Supreme Court ruling allowed same-sex marriage. In 2015 PrideFest, a successor to small Gay Pride events of four decades earlier, attracted some 350,000 people.

The People in 2015

In 2015 many residents of the metropolitan area had little memory of the tensions of the 1960s and 1970s. Health problems in 1987 sidelined Corky Gonzales. He died in 2005, and Rachel Noel passed away at age ninety in 2008. Many black and Hispanic activists faded or, like journalist George Brown, who became Colorado's lieutenant governor in 1974, became mainstream leaders when they won political office. Less overtly racist and more integrated in 2015 than it had been a half century earlier, Denver was still a place with economic divides between its more affluent white residents, who tended to live in its eastern, southeastern, and southwestern neighborhoods; its Hispanic citizens, who concentrated in areas west of the South Platte River; and its black residents, many of whom lived in far northeastern neighborhoods, such as Montbello. By an odd twist of fate, Five Points and nearby Curtis Park, once the locus of most of the city's black population, was by 2015 an increasingly white gentrified area of restored old homes complemented by upscale new construction, well served by public transportation, much as it had been 135 years earlier when it initially sprouted as Denver's first streetcar suburb.

By 2015 the saga of Denver's people could no longer be told in terms of the ethnic neighborhoods and struggles of 1910 or 1970. Instead, it was a metropolitan-wide story that embraced a heterogeneous population with representatives from most of the countries of the world.

According to *American Fact Finder,* a US Census online service, in the 2008–13 period the metropolis embraced people of Egyptian, Syrian, Basque, Brazilian, Dutch, Finnish, Korean, Nigerian, Sudanese, Danish, Portuguese, Ukrainian, Italian, Ethiopian, Swiss, Lebanese, Belgian, Yugoslavian, Scottish, Romanian, Lithuanian, Latvian, Greek, and scores of other ancestries. Aurora in particular became a magnet for Latinos and blacks, a haven for refugees, and a United Nations of peoples. It also became home in the 1980s to the Aurora Detention Facility at 3130 North Oakland Street. That three-hundred-thousand-square-foot privately run prison, with space for more than fifteen hundred captives, gives the US Immigration and Customs Enforcement a place to keep people before deporting many of them.

Central to the story of the metro area's people in recent decades has been the burgeoning Hispanic population. In 1910 few people of Hispanic ancestry lived in Denver, and even in 1960 the number was fewer than 50,000. Census estimates for 2010 put the population of people with Hispanic or Latino roots in Denver at 190,965 (32 percent of the total population), in Aurora at 93,363 (29 percent), and in Lakewood at 31,467 (22 percent). Northern suburbs such as Thornton and Commerce City tended to have large number of Hispanics; southern places such as Centennial, Greenwood Village, and Littleton had far fewer. When former congressman and Littleton resident Tom Tancredo, well known for his efforts to restrict immigration, ran for Colorado governor in 2010, he found considerable support in Douglas County suburbs and much less in Denver County.

The smooth integration of a large number of Latinos into the broader society continues to challenge the region, which can take some comfort in knowing that for more than a century and a half Denver, despite periodic attacks of racism and xenophobia, has cobbled together a society in which diverse people usually get along. However, divided by national origins, by religion, by political affiliations, by class and money, and sometimes by language, the people of Greater Denver have continually struggled to find common ground and a sense of community. Thanks to the city's sports teams, many of them, in a limited way, did.

Chapter Thirteen

A Sporting Town

ounded by mostly young males, Denver started out and has remained attractive to young folks who tend to enjoy participating
in or watching sports. In 1865 local Germans established a Turnverein to
foster physical fitness and sport. Another early promoter of sports, the
Denver Athletic Club (DAC), opened in 1884. The club built a gym where
it encouraged physical fitness and sponsored horse racing, bicycling, and
other recreation. In 1890 the DAC created an outdoor sports complex, the
DAC Park, where East High School's athletic fields now are, at York Street
and East Seventeenth Avenue. On November 15, 1890, the DAC inaugu-
rated the park with a football game against the University of Colorado,
crushing CU 34–0. Throughout the 1890s, the DAC regularly defeated college and athletic clubs but dropped the team in 1905 after a scandalous
revelation that it was paying its supposedly amateur players.

Football would become the most popular spectator sport in a town
that often gets rated among the nation's most athletically minded cities. Personal physical fitness is also big business. On Sunday mornings,
many Denverites work out in a health club rather than go to church. On
Sunday and Saturday afternoons, residents will typically be found watching the city's many major league teams or out biking, hiking, golfing, or
skiing. Denver boasts more professional teams than any other city in the
country. Baseball, basketball, football, hockey, outdoor and indoor lacrosse, rugby, and soccer teams play in six state-of-the-art, metro-area
stadiums (Broomfield's Events Center, Coors Field, Dick's Sporting
Goods Park in Commerce City, Infinity Park in Glendale, Pepsi Center,
and Mile High Stadium).

The Denver Broncos

Broncomania has become Denver's major sports fever. This American Football League team started out in 1960 with four wins, nine losses, and a tie. Despite enthusiastic fan support, the Broncos regularly lost five games for every one they won. The team had little to brag about until 1967, when they hired Floyd Little, an All-American running back from Syracuse University. Little was little—just five-foot-ten and 195 pounds—but the first Bronco giant. He played until 1975 and led professional football in rushing for six of those years. After becoming part of the National Football League (NFL) in 1970, the Broncos finally battled to their first winning season in 1973, with seven wins, five losses, and two ties. Rabid fans of the orange and blue began buying a bumper sticker proclaiming: "IF GOD ISN'T A BRONCO FAN WHY ARE SUNSETS ORANGE AND BLUE?"

Prayers of devout fans brought a miracle to the Mile High City in 1977. That year NFL veteran quarterback Craig Morton joined the team, finally giving the Broncos a consistent quarterback. That same lucky year, owner Gerald Phipps hired a new coach, Red Miller. Miller won team respect after he got down on the line of scrimmage in practice to demonstrate blocking techniques. Even after a collision with monster tackle Claudie Minor resulted in a bloody gash on his left eye, Miller stayed on the field. Players took to a coach who would butt heads with them, bleeding or not.

The Denver Athletic Club regularly outscored the University of Colorado in one of Denver's earliest football rivalries. In this Thanksgiving Day 1899 contest, the DAC team is on its way to yet another win over the Buffaloes. Courtesy Tom Noel Collection.

Morton and Miller led the team to their first Super Bowl. When the offense sputtered, the aggressive "Orange Crush" defense not only stopped the enemy but also often forced turnovers and scored on some of them. That magical season came to a dismal end in the 1978 Super Bowl showdown with the Dallas Cowboys, which the Broncos lost 27–10. Despite the defeat, Broncomania became embedded in Colorado. Priests rescheduled masses around the Sunday ritual held in the high holy place of Mile High Stadium. BMH Synagogue ordered orange yarmulkes. When the Broncos were in the January NFL playoffs, attendance suffered at the National Western Stock Show. Denver's City and County Building switched from Christmas red and green outdoor lighting to orange and blue.

Denver businessmen Gerald and Allan Phipps, sons of the millionaire US senator Lawrence C. Phipps, hung on to the team until 1981, when they sold it for a reported $40 million to Edgar J. Kaiser Jr., the grandson of industrialist and Kaiser Permanente HMO founder Henry J. Kaiser. In 1983 Kaiser and his new head coach, Dan Reeves, secured the team's future when they acquired a rookie quarterback named John Elway. The following year Kaiser transferred ownership to Patrick Bowlen—reportedly for $70 million, a figure that made the Broncos the NFL's most valuable franchise. Dyed-in-the-orange-and-blue fans and consistently sold-out seasons attested to Colorado's crazy love of the Broncos, win or lose.

Mostly they won—only to stumble in the end. In the 1987 showdown against the New York Giants, the Broncos' first Super Bowl appearance with John Elway as quarterback, the team went down 39–20. The following year, Super Bowl XXII saw the Washington Redskins flail Denver 42–10. Even more humiliation came in 1990, with a 55–10 knockout delivered by the San Francisco 49ers. Four previous Super Bowl losses were forgiven in 1998 when the Broncos defeated the Green Bay Packers 31–24. Denver staged a giant victory celebration. Hundreds of thousands lined Seventeenth Street to cheer the hometown heroes, who waved back from atop fire engines creeping through a blizzard of confetti in the city's largest-ever parade. In 1999 the Broncos again made it to the Super Bowl and shot down the Atlanta Falcons, led by former Broncos head coach Dan Reeves, 34–19.

John Elway retired after that Super Bowl game, and the Broncos went back to being good, but not Super Bowl good. Yet hopeful fans who "bleed orange" cheered nail-biting, heart-stopping, last-minute heroics that snatched victories from defeat or vice versa. Ironically, the Broncos played more poorly for their first ten years in the new Mile High Stadium than in the old. Hopes and prayers for another Super Bowl arrived in 2012 with a later version of Elway, quarterback Peyton Manning. His passing game took the team to the 2014 Super Bowl, where they suffered a lopsided loss to the Seattle Seahawks. That fall Manning broke the all-time record for most passing touchdowns and strove to get the team back into the Super Bowl. As has been the case for decades, every Bronco game sold out, and scalpers asked $1,000 and more for fifty-yard-line seats.

Tickets sold for even more in 2016, although the Broncos were the underdog in Super Bowl L (50). Denver's defense deflated the high-flying, undefeated Carolina Panthers, 24–10. Manning retired afterward, but defensive stars led by Von Miller sparked Mile High hopes for more national championships to come.

Mile High Stadium

The Broncos had first played in Bears Stadium, which they shared with the city's Minor League Baseball team, the Denver Bears. Huge football crowds and often sold-out games led to the transformation of Bears Stadium, which initially seated seventeen thousand, into seventy-six-thousand-seat Mile High Stadium—a hybrid football-baseball venue. The city of Denver took all revenue from Mile High Stadium parking, concessions, and advertising in return for covering operations and maintenance. Phipps had sold off to private owners another cash cow—about $3 million annual rental on the sixty luxury skyboxes. Bowlen wanted those dollars and undertook to convince voters to build a new stadium, where he could pocket the income streams.

Bowlen, as historian James Whiteside recounts in *Colorado: A Sports History*, argued that he needed more income so he could recruit top players to field a championship team. He hinted that economic reality might force him to sell to an owner who might not have a strong commitment to Denver. Little matter that Roman coliseums stood for

two thousand years and that engineers judged Mile High Stadium struc-
turally sound. Fearful that their team might relocate or sink into medi-
ocrity, metro-area voters in 1999 agreed to extend the .01 percent sales
tax that had funded Coors Field so the Broncos could build a grand
new home. *Rocky Mountain News* columnist Gene Amole observed that
taxpayers "rarely have enough money to attend the games themselves.
We often hear about limiting welfare for the poor. How about limiting
welfare for the rich too?" City councilman Dennis Gallagher found it
"ironic to devote $188 million in tax revenue to millionaires of society
while we lift a sneering lip to the welfare mother in the food line."

To build a new Mile High Stadium next to the old, the Broncos cor-
ralled not only sales-tax financing but also $120 million that Invesco, a
mutual funds company, paid for the naming rights. Public protest about
losing the Mile High name led to a compromise—the new home of the
Broncos became officially Invesco Field at Mile High. After Invesco gave
up the rights, Sports Authority, the largest Colorado sporting-goods
chain, bought the naming rights. In 2001, with the new stadium in place,
the old one, scene of thousands of baseball games, hundreds of football
matches, assorted rock concerts, a Billy Graham revival, and a massively
attended Mass celebrated by Pope John Paul II during World Youth Day
of 1993, was razed.

The new Mile High Stadium also hosts lacrosse, which started as
a Native American ball-and-stick game and began enthralling tens of
thousands of Coloradans in 2006 with the Denver Outlaws of Major
League Lacrosse (MLL). Their first game set the MLL attendance record of
13,167. In 2011 the Outlaws set another attendance record of 27,184 at their
July 3 game. Coloradans, it seemed, outdid the nation in attending even
lesser-known sporting competitions such as lacrosse.

Baseball

Denverites have cheered baseball players ever since 1862, when the *Rocky
Mountain News* first reported the score of a game. In 1900 the Denver
Bears became the state's first well-known professional team. By 1955 the
Bears thrived as a farm franchise for the powerful New York Yankees,
and in 1957 they took the top spot in the Junior World Series. While
supporting their Minor Leaguers, fans also chased big-league baseball

dreams. The longtime fantasy came true in 1993 when the Colorado Rockies, a National League expansion team, began playing in Denver. In their first home game, April 9, 1993, lead-off batter Eric Young hit a home run.

Two years later the Rockies moved from Mile High Stadium to their own ballpark, Coors Field. It cost $215 million, raised with a .01 percent sales tax approved by 54 percent of metro-area voters. The Coors Brewing Company pitched in another $30 million to have the stadium named for the state's longtime major suds maker. Located at Twentieth and Blake Streets, the field transformed the area into a district of sports bars. Designed with traditional architectural ballpark elements, including a vintage brick-and-stone exterior, the facility blended into the adjacent Lower Downtown and Ball Park Historic Districts.

Rockies mania quickly developed into a civic obsession, second only to Broncomania. Even before the Rockies occupied Coors Field, they set a Major League attendance record by filling nearly 4.5 million Mile High Stadium seats in the course of the 1993 season. They earned the nickname the "Blake Street Bombers" because the thin Mile High air makes it easier to hit long balls. However, because finding pitchers who can throw effectively has been a perennial problem for the Rockies, visiting hitters often outslug the home team. Fans cheered, chanted, and stomped their feet for the likes of Larry Walker, the first Rocky to win the National League's Most Valuable Player Award. This Canadian slugger joined the Colorado Rockies (1995–2004) as their right fielder. In 1997 Walker batted .366 with 49 home runs, 130 runs batted in, 33 stolen bases, and 409 total hits to win that MVP Award. After Walker, first baseman Todd Helton and shortstop Troy Tulowitzki stepped up to the plate with game-winning hits that led the Rockies to the National League championship in 2007. Their hopes of a World Series win collapsed when they lost to the Boston Red Sox.

Basketball

Before becoming director of Denver's YMCA, basketball's inventor, James Naismith, had yearned for an indoor winter sport. In 1891 he invented the game in Massachusetts, and it quickly bounced into popularity. Folks rigged up bushel baskets, wastebaskets—any kind of baskets—and started shooting. Under the auspices of the Amateur Athletic Union, basketball flourished as Colorado's first great indoor spectator sport. The old AAU Denver Nuggets evolved into an American Basketball Association professional team (1970–76) and then a National Basketball Association (NBA) franchise of the same name.

Before 1972 local basketballers experimented with other names and other leagues. Once they were the Piggly Wigglies, sometimes called the Pigs, thanks to their sponsor, the Piggly Wiggly grocery chain. In 1967 the Denver Larks, named after the Colorado state bird (lark bunting), failed to fly for a second season. Denver trucking magnate Bill Ringsby bought the birds for $350,000 and renamed them the Rockets, after his company's long-haul truck logo. In 1972 he sold the team to San Diego businessmen Frank Goldberg and A. G. "Bud" Fisher, who restored the Denver Nuggets name. With the acquisition of coach Larry Brown and shooting stars Dan Issel and David Thompson, the team made the American Basketball Association finals in 1975–76 and moved up to the top-tier National Basketball Association. There the Nuggets continued to win division titles but advanced no further.

David Thompson, the Nuggets' superstar, was nicknamed "Skywalker" for his vertical leaps, for his alley-oop, above-the-rim passes, and for starring in the first NBA Slam Dunk Contests. He played in Denver from 1975 to 1982, shining as an NBA All-Star for four years and leading the Nuggets to the NBA playoffs in 1978. Once the highest-paid player in the NBA, he succumbed to the substance abuse that haunts professional sports. Only after it ended his career did he overcome his cocaine addiction.

Another Nugget became an exemplary role model, both on and off the court. Alexander English starred from 1979 to 1990. At his peak, he was the NBA's top scorer and a frequent All-Star. Off the court, he acted in movies, wrote poetry, and pursued philanthropic causes. Dan "the Horse" Issel excelled as a Nugget from 1975 to 1985. Returning as head coach in 1992, he transformed a lackluster franchise into a 1994 playoff contender. His career crashed in 2001 when he slung an ethnic slur at a taunting Hispanic fan and subsequently resigned under pressure. During the 2000s, the Nuggets became the talk of the town because of the great play of hometown star Chauncey Billups and the glamorous Carmelo Anthony until 2011, when they were traded away.

As more and more fans showed up, the hoopsters yearned for a grander home. That came in 1975 with the opening of city-owned McNichols Arena, near Mile High Stadium. In a town where money seemed to be no obstacle when it came to sports facilities, McNichols, which seated nearly seventeen thousand and cost $16 million, was replaced with the $180 million Pepsi Center, near Speer Boulevard and Auraria Parkway, in 1999. The public did not have to foot the bill for the Pepsi Center, which, although it enjoyed property-tax breaks, was built with private money. The Nuggets and the Pepsi Center found big-league financing in Kroenke Sports Enterprises, which bought the team and the Pepsi Center in 2000. Founder-owner Stan Kroenke, a son-in-law of Walmart cofounder Bud Walton, in partnership with his son, Josh, had deep pockets. The Kroenkes also owned the Colorado Rapids of Major League Soccer, the Colorado Mammoth of the National Lacrosse League, and the Colorado Avalanche of the National Hockey League.

Hockey

In the mid-1990s the Colorado Avalanche swept hockey fans off their feet. That National Hockey League franchise had started out as the Quebec Nordiques before moving to Colorado in 1995. The Avalanche fared better than had earlier hockey teams, the Denver Falcons, the Denver Mavericks, the Denver Invaders, the Denver Grizzlies, the Rangers, and others. Most of them melted in a year or less. More durable were the Western Hockey League's Denver Spurs (1968–76) and the National Hockey League's Colorado Rockies, which played in Denver from 1976 to 1982 before moving to New Jersey to become the Devils.

During their first ten years in Denver, the Avalanche rolled with eight division titles and went to the playoffs. They became the only NHL team to win the Stanley Cup their first season after a relocation. Besides that 1996 triumph, the Avalanche won the cup again in 2001. Among the team's stars, Peter Forsberg, Joe Sakic, and Patrick Roy shined brightest. The Swedish-born Forsberg was named the NHL's most valuable player for his performance in 2003–4. Canadian-born team captain Joe Sakic

Captain Joe Sakic and the Colorado Avalanche celebrated their National Hockey League Championship in 2001 that brought the Stanley Cup to Denver. Courtesy VISIT DENVER.

achieved supernova status and also starred off the ice with his work with high school hockey teams and the homeless.

The team's anchor in those glory years was a Quebec City native, Patrick Jacques Roy. He began playing goalie at age seven and joined various Canadian ice hockey teams, including the Montreal Canadiens. In 1995 he played the opening season with the Colorado Avalanche and emerged as their biggest star. His celebrity status helped make Denver a hockey town. Roy's signature style, known as the butterfly, where he knelt on the ice with his legs at right angles to his body, is physically impossible for most mortals. His flexibility enabled him to cover the entire bottom of the net with his leg pads, reducing the number of goals scored against the Avalanche. Roy played in Denver until his retirement in 2003. In 2012 the team brought him back as head coach, adding Joe Sakic in 2013 as executive vice president of hockey operations.

Soccer and Rugby

Kroenke Sports brought big-league soccer to Denver in 1995 when the Colorado Rapids became one of Major League Soccer's ten original franchises. The Rapids ran at Mile High Stadium before moving in 2007 to a state-of-the-art soccer stadium—Dick's Sporting Goods Park—in

Commerce City. This eighteen-thousand-seat venue surrounded by a twenty-four-field soccer complex on a 917-acre site was built by a public-private partnership between Kroenke Sports Enterprises and Commerce City. The Rapids rapidly popularized soccer. More and more local schools adopted this sport, which requires less equipment, allows more running time, and produces fewer injuries than football. Soccer is played by both sexes and is friendly to normal-size people, unlike basketball and football, where height and size give big bruisers an advantage. Newcomers from Europe and Latin America were particularly pleased to see the city embracing the world's most popular sport.

Rugby also rooted itself in Denver. Infinity Park opened in 2007 as home for the major-league Glendale Raptors. This grassy new heart for the town of Glendale, an enclave completely surrounded by Denver, encompasses an events center, sports complex, public gardens, water features, picnic areas, a field house, an outdoor pavilion, a rugby practice field, and a planned waterfront park along Cherry Creek. Infinity Park hosted the 2009 Churchill Cup Rugby Pool, the leading international tournament, which draws teams from seven nations. Well aware that the biggest money in sports comes from television, Stan Kroenke established Altitude Sports and Entertainment in 2004. This Rocky Mountain regional network broadcasts the majority of Avalanche, Nuggets, and Rapids games as well as other athletic events and Pepsi Center music concerts. Kroenke Sports Enterprises also ventured into vintage theaters with its acquisition and operation of Denver's grand old movie palace, the Paramount.

Rodeo

Horses galore still perform in one major sport that survives in county fairgrounds and at some high schools and colleges, not to mention the National Western Stock Show. Modern rodeo traces its origins to an 1869 competition in Deer Trail, a tiny town in eastern Arapahoe County. Pro Rodeo came to Denver with the National Western Stock Show, which launches the annual season for the Professional Rodeo Cowboy Association circuit. Catering to the 20 percent of Coloradans claiming Hispanic origins and to honor the Hispanic origins of rodeo, the stock show in 1994 launched a Mexican Rodeo Extravaganza, complete with a Sunday

National Western Stock Show attractions such as Jerry Diaz and the Mexican Rodeo Extravaganza draw January crowds to Denver who relish its cow-town heritage. Denver voters in 2015 approved a massive upgrade and expansion of the stock show grounds to make it a year-round attraction. Courtesy Tom Noel Collection.

mariachi Mass. Rodeo bucked up attendance at what had started out in 1906 as a livestock exhibition and horse show. By the 2000s, the stock show attracted some six hundred thousand visitors for the sixteen-day show in mid-January.

Skiing

With marketing that lured vacationers from around the world, skiing snowballed into the single most important segment of Colorado's tourist industry, accounting for roughly one in seven of the state's tourist-related jobs. Since 1990 the Highest State has averaged at least ten million skiers a year. Denver, as the airport of choice and the home of Ski Country USA, capitalized on skiing to promote winter tourism.

Although some Denverites enjoyed skiing on the gentle slopes at Genesee Park, a city-owned mountain park, in the 1920s, and on the challenging terrain at Berthoud Pass and Winter Park in the 1930s and 1940s, it was not until after World War II that city residents by the thousands flocked to some of the best ski resorts in the nation at Aspen and Vail. Both owed much of their early development to veterans of the US Army's Tenth Mountain Division, who trained at Camp Hale, near

Leadville, during the war. Peter Seibert, who overcame his war injuries to again become an expert skier, joined partners in 1957 to buy a 520-acre ranch on the west side of Vail Pass. They obtained a Forest Service permit allowing them to build trails on federal land. In December 1962, Vail opened with the country's first gondola, ten miles of trails, a small restaurant, a gas station, and parking for 650 cars.

By the early 1990s, Vail, which had expanded to include Beaver Creek, added Arrowhead (1993) and took over Ralston Purina's Arapahoe Basin, Keystone, and Breckenridge ski areas. Vail Associates, as historian James Whiteside reported, became "the unrivaled skiing giant of Colorado and the United States." Renamed Vail Resorts in 1996, it has grown to include intensely developed ski areas, helping create a mountain corridor along I-70 more densely populated in spots than many Front Range cities. From its Broomfield headquarters, Vail Resorts has expanded to include ski areas in Utah, the Grand Tetons, and Lake Tahoe.

As historian William Philpott points out in his book *Vacationland: Tourism and the Environment in the Colorado High Country,* Denverites invested heavily in the ski industry and other mountain recreation. The City of Denver built and still owns Winter Park Ski Area, a popular part of the Denver Mountain Park system. The Denver and Rio Grande Western Railroad for decades ran a ski train from Denver's Union Station to Winter Park. With early access not only by rail but also by US 40 (paved in 1938) over Berthoud Pass, Winter Park became a Denver favorite. As Philpott notes, the post–World War II boom in mountain homes, condos, and time-shares at Winter Park and along the I-70 mountain corridor has extended Denver's suburban lifestyle into the mountains west of town.

Mountaineering

With many of the nation's most spectacular mountains in their backyard, Denverites are naturally tempted to climb them. The most ambitious mountaineers aim to conquer all fifty-four of the state's 14,000-foot peaks. Many brag of their accomplishments, but few, if any, can match the record of unassuming Denver attorney Jim Gehres, who by 2003 had summited all the fourteeners at least twelve times. Less energetic folks can drive to the top of 14,265-foot Mount Evans and 14,110-foot Pikes Peak. Ever since 1912, Denver's Colorado Mountain Club (CMC) has been promoting mountain recreation and offering hiking, climbing, snow-shoeing, and skiing trips. In 1993 the CMC joined with the American Alpine Club (AAC) to purchase and renovate the elegant but abandoned Golden High School. The AAC then moved its headquarters from New York City into what has become the American Mountaineering Center. Along with the Golden headquarters of the AAC, CMC, and Outward Bound, the center has a 350-seat auditorium, the largest US mountaineering library, a museum, and a climbing wall. Even the most city-bound Denverites fancy the snowcapped Rockies, which lift spirits and promise exhilarating escape from urban routines.

Cycling

At least as early as 1869, a few Denverites were riding "velocipedes." A little more than a decade later, the city council, concerned because cyclists scared horses, almost banned the use of the contraptions for anyone over the age of twelve. Such naysaying did no good. By the 1880s citizens were organizing riding clubs, and in the 1890s the city ranked high among the most bicycle-loving places in the country. Then, as an organized sport, cycling went into semihibernation for more than sixty years. Several famous Colorado races and a renewed commitment to health and the environment helped revive the sport. Since 1972 Durango's annual Iron Horse Classic has pitted cyclists against the Durango-Silverton narrow-gauge steam train. Other annual events, such as the *Denver Post's* "Ride the Rockies," also attract thousands.

In 2011 Colorado began hosting America's answer to the Tour de France, the USA Pro Cycling Challenger Race, through spectacular, rugged mountain terrain. The event drew nearly a million fans and sparked an estimated $83.5 million in economic activity. Rising parking fees also fostered cycling, as did support from the state and local governments. Denver in 2009 launched one of the nation's first large-scale, citywide bike-sharing systems, with five hundred rentable red bikes at more than fifty stations. Boulder and other communities hosted similar programs.

Golf

Overland Park in Denver opened as Colorado's first golf course in 1896. Today the state offers more than three hundred public and private courses. Metro Denver's foremost courses, Castle Pines and Cherry Hills, have hosted national and international tournaments. They and other upscale golf havens, such as the Denver and Columbine Country Clubs, have become the centerpieces for posh residential neighborhoods and playgrounds of the wealthy elite. From the beginning, both sexes enjoyed the game. Many have forgotten that Denver's most famous golfer was a woman—Mildred "Babe" Didrikson Zaharias. "America's greatest woman athlete," according to *The Official Encyclopedia of Sports,* played on the All-American Women's Basketball Team (1930–32) and won gold medals at the 1932 Olympic Games in the 80-meter hurdles and the javelin throw. She married George Zaharias, a professional wrestler known as "the amazing Greek from Cripple Creek," in 1938 and moved to Denver. There she took up golf and won the 1946 Women's Amateur title and seventeen other amateur titles in a row, including the British Open. As a professional, she won the US Women's Open in 1948, 1950, and 1954. Even after being stricken with cancer, Babe continued to play until her death in 1956.

More Mile High Sports Stars

Besides Zaharias, Denver over the years has had many other local sports figures to admire. Cyclist Dora Ellen Rinehart racked up seventeen thousand miles in 1896 and gained national attention for making twenty hundred-mile "century" rides in twenty days. In his *Colorado: A Sports History,* James Whiteside notes that on Sundays Rinehart took relaxed spins with her husband because, as she said, "it does take so much starch out of a man to ride a century." Another top athlete, Phyllis Lockwood, spent much of her career in Boulder from 1935 until emphysema ended her career in 1970. A standout in tennis, basketball, track and field, swimming, and softball, she reigned as Colorado's singles tennis champ, played for Denver's AAU women's basketball teams for eighteen years, and became a basketball All-American in 1949.

One of the first African Americans inducted into the Colorado Sports Hall of Fame, Jerome Cousins Biffle attended Denver's East High School. After winning all-state honors in the 100- and 220-yard sprints, high jump, and broad jump, he went to the University of Denver (DU). At DU Biffle was known as "the one-man track team." In 1950 he captured first-place finishes in collegiate track, won the National Collegiate Athletic Association long-jump title, and was named *Track and Field News*'s top collegiate track star. At the 1952 Summer Olympics, held in Helsinki, Finland, he won a gold medal in the long jump. He returned home to coach track for many years at East High School. Another Olympian, seventeen-year-old swimmer Missy (Melissa) Franklin of the Denver suburb of Centennial, gained international fame in the 2012 London Summer Olympics, where she won four gold medals and one bronze.

Denver's mountain backdrop, many sporting venues, and recreational opportunities have all added to its appeal. Without question, sports have provided much of the glue that holds the metropolitan area together. Baseball, football, soccer fields, Stanley Cups, and Super Bowl triumphs have, however, been only one of the factors giving the region a sense of identity. Denverites have also used historic preservation, museums, libraries, and public art to build community.

Chapter Fourteen

Preservation Pacesetters

$\mathcal{H}$ ow will we know it's us without our past?," a question posed in John Steinbeck's *The Grapes of Wrath,* has become increasingly relevant in Denver and its suburbs over the past half century. Having lost many of its architectural and historical treasures between 1955 and 1975, the city risked losing its identity. Goaded by preservationists, it gradually came to appreciate its heritage. The suburbs, overwhelmed by rapid growth, also recognized that their pasts could provide them with a sense of community. Likewise, the city and its suburbs have come to value historical museums, research facilities, and public art because those things, like the Denver Broncos and the Colorado Rockies, knit together a disparate collection of Front Range communities.

Historic Preservation

Historic preservation had few advocates during Denver's first hundred years. Pioneers built rude log cabins and soon replaced them with substantial brick houses that they demolished to construct commercial buildings. Jerome Smiley in his monumental 1901 *History of Denver* noted that some downtown locations had seen three and even four different buildings during the city's first forty-three years. Some buildings survived simply by virtue of inertia or lucky accident. One of the city's oldest structures, now much altered, known as the Wells Fargo Depot on the southeast corner of Fifteenth and Market Streets, dates to around 1874, and some of it may go back to the 1860s. Spared commercial pressure because it was far from the city's center, Four Mile House at 715 South Forest Street, a stop for travelers on their way into Denver, retains sections from 1859, making it the city's oldest building. Frozen in time, the Byers-Evans house on the northeast corner of Bannock Street and

West Fourteenth Avenue persisted because the Evans family continued to live there long after practically everyone else in their social class had moved farther east. Pioneer editor William N. Byers built the house in 1883 and sold it in 1889 to William Gray Evans, son of former territorial governor John Evans. It stayed in the Evans family until the 1980s, when it was donated to the Colorado Historical Society, which made it into a house museum, a semisleeper among better-known nearby attractions, such as the Denver Art Museum.

Margaret "Molly" Brown gets credit as one of Denver's first preservationists. In 1927 she saved the cottage of poet and journalist Eugene Field, which stood at 307 West Colfax Avenue. Relocated to Washington Park, it served for many years as a branch of the Denver Public Library. Wealthy May Bonfils Stanton took pity on a pioneer Auraria cabin and had it moved to her Belmar estate. After May died, the little cabin made its way to the History Colorado Center.

Without guardian angels such as Brown and Bonfils to protect them, it is amazing that as late as 1959, when Denver celebrated the centennial of the 1859 gold rush, many of its great old buildings still survived. The Windsor Hotel on the northwest corner of Eighteenth and Larimer Streets, the city's finest when it opened in June 1880, had sunk into seediness. The Tabor Grand Opera House (1881), its interior gutted in the early 1920s to convert it to a movie theater, remained at Sixteenth and Curtis Streets. Next to it, on the southeast corner of Sixteenth and Arapahoe Streets, the Old Customs House, a solid, sooty government building built in the 1880s, still stood. A block away the Mining Exchange Building (1891), topped by a statue of a miner, dominated the southeast corner of Fifteenth and Arapahoe Streets.

By the early 1970s, the Tabor, the Windsor, the Mining Exchange, and the Old Customs House were gone. Gone too were most of the other buildings in the midsection of downtown. The Mining Exchange made way for Brooks Tower, which saved the miner and put him in its entry plaza. Rubble from the Tabor and the Old Customs House was trucked away to make room for the Denver Branch of the Federal Reserve Bank, and the Windsor site eventually became home to Sunset Park, low-income apartments run by the Volunteers of America. The commercial pressures that erased the Mining Exchange, the Tabor, and the

Windsor would have slowly eroded much of the rest of old downtown had it not been for the Denver Urban Renewal Authority (DURA), which in the late 1960s and 1970s, armed with the power of eminent domain, destroyed in a few years what would have taken private developers decades. DURA cleared more than a hundred acres, removing 625 businesses and thousands of people. It spared only a few structures, such as the Daniels and Fisher tower at Sixteenth and Arapahoe Streets and the Denver City Cable Railway powerhouse and offices at Eighteenth and Lawrence Streets. To save downtown, DURA argued, it had to destroy part of it.

Some people disagreed. In 1965 developer Dana Crawford and others formed Larimer Square Associates to preserve and revitalize Larimer Street, between Fourteenth and Fifteenth Streets. Denver's main business street in the 1870s, Larimer had by the 1930s become a part of the city's skid row, a boon to preservationists because developers with better opportunities elsewhere shunned the street. Crawford and her associates gambled and won. By the late 1960s, Larimer Square's shops and restaurants demonstrated that preservation worked. That successful start led to the revitalization of much of Lower Downtown.

Americans grew more concerned about their venerable buildings in the 1960s, thanks in part to Jacqueline Kennedy, whose restoration of the White House caught the public's imagination. Lady Bird Johnson also pushed historic preservation, and in 1966 President Lyndon Johnson signed the National Historic Preservation Act, which created a National Register of Historic Places and provided federal money for preservation. In 1967 Denver established a Landmark Preservation Commission, which became a bulwark against the destruction of many structures. Three years later, fearing that the Molly Brown House at 1340 Pennsylvania Street might be razed, citizens formed Historic Denver, Inc., which raised money to buy Brown's House of Lions, so called for the twin statues that adorned its entrance, and turn it into a house museum. In the early seventies, Historic Denver, led by Barbara Sudler and assisted by Barbara Norgren, rescued and restored a block of Victorian-era houses on Ninth Street as part of the Auraria Higher Education Center, thereby giving what might have become a sterile urban campus a charming island of greenery and vintage homes. The 1984 formation of Colorado Preservation, Inc., brought additional statewide clout to the preservation movement.

Dana Crawford launched Denver's vibrant preservation movement by saving Larimer Square during the 1960s. Its success inspired a much greater preservation triumph in Lower Downtown between Cherry Creek and Twentieth Street from Larimer to Wynkoop Streets. Photo by Jim Milmoe, courtesy Tom Noel Collection.

The champions of bygone days did not win every battle. They failed to save one of the city's grandest mansions, entrepreneur David H. Moffat's home on the northeast corner of East Eighth Avenue and Logan Street, which was wrecked in 1970. They could not rescue the classy Central Bank Building at Fifteenth and Arapahoe Streets, demolished in 1989. They did, however, gradually raise public appreciation of historical and architectural treasures. That appreciation in turn helped them develop the political muscle they needed to preserve thousands of buildings by securing state tax credits for those maintaining historic structures. They also got, in the course of a quarter century, more than $250 million for preservation by hitching their star to a mighty economic engine. In 1990 voters passed a Colorado constitutional amendment legalizing casino gambling in Black Hawk, Central City, and Cripple Creek, with part of the taxes going to preservation. As of 2015, the State Historical Fund had financed some four thousand projects across all sixty-four counties and put $47 million into the state capitol restoration project finally completed in 2015.

A national preservation pacesetter, Denver had by 2015 more than 330 individually designated landmarks and had protected thousands of other structures in its fifty-two landmark districts. Preservation has succeeded because it makes economic sense. By protecting some of the city's poshest neighborhoods to the east of downtown, Denver ensured that a goodly number of its wealthier citizens would continue to pay city property taxes and to take an interest in its well-being. Also, because it promoted upscale development near downtown, preservation contributed to the health of the city's core.

The Lower Downtown Historic District provides a prime example of preservation success. The neighborhood bounded by Cherry Creek and Twentieth Street, between Larimer and Wynkoop Streets, once the heart of the city, had become Denver's skid row by the 1930s. After historic-district designation in 1988, LoDo began to be transformed. Coors Field opened on the edge of LoDo in 1995. Sensitive architects made the ballpark blend into its surroundings by sinking it into the ground to keep it the same height as neighboring warehouses and by building it in brick, as the warehouses were. Sage entrepreneurs transformed ramshackle nearby structures into lofts, art galleries, brewpubs,

The Lower Downtown Historic District has become a model for transforming skid rows into thriving loft, restaurant, and entertainment havens. Photo by Tom Noel.

restaurants, and nightclubs. Dime beers and quarter shots have been replaced by $7 beers and $10 shots. Dollar-a-night flophouses have given way to million-dollar lofts. In 1999 art patrons Frederick and Jan Mayer built their multimillion-dollar Red House in the neighborhood. In 2015, Union Station, the area's anchor, was reinvented. That icon's rebirth as a hive of restaurants, bars, shops, and the upper-floor Crawford Hotel encouraged construction of more than a dozen nearby high-rise residences and office towers. Union Station and its adjacent rail yards, forlorn, forgotten, and depopulated for decades, now rank among the most densely populated sections of the metropolitan area. LoDo has become a model for how a city can transform a dangerous, declining skid row into a high-end district and playground for an entire metro area. Thousands of suburbanites pour into LoDo for ballgames and a night on the town. Young and old enjoy a respite from standard suburban retail districts. Consciously or subconsciously, these visitors come to appreciate historic preservation.

Metro Museums

Denver has long used museums to promote and preserve its past, to create greater historical awareness, and to attract tourists. Proud pioneers formed the Colorado Pioneers Society in 1866, when the city was only eight years old. In 1879 some of them created the State Historical and Natural History Society. In the early 1900s, the historians and natural historians parted company and settled in different homes. The Denver Museum of Natural History (today's Denver Museum of Nature and Science) constructed its museum at the east end of City Park. The Colorado Historical Society built a Greek temple of Colorado Yule marble on East Fourteenth Avenue, just south of the state capitol. That museum has evolved into today's History Colorado Center, on East Twelfth Avenue and Broadway. Two of History Colorado's eleven regional museums are in Denver. The Byers-Evans House Museum focuses on Denver history and the two families most important in shaping the city, while the Pearce-McAllister Cottage has morphed into the Denver Museum of Miniatures, Dolls and Toys.

Denver's Capitol Hill mansions, as historian Louisa Ward Arps notes in her classic *Denver in Slices,* "were as vigorous in design and

generous in proportion as the whiskers of the men who paid for them." Many of those mansions have been preserved as museums, including the Denver Botanic Gardens House, the Governor's Residence, the Molly Brown House, and the Pearce-McAllister Cottage, all

History Colorado at 1200 Broadway welcomes museumgoers, researchers, preservationists, archaeologists, and tourists. Courtesy History Colorado.

of which welcome tourists. On Cherry Creek, the Four Mile House has been preserved as the hub of a living history museum. The Forney Museum of Transportation at 4303 Brighton Boulevard boasts more than five hundred vehicles, from stagecoaches to limousines. Winged vehicles are showcased in the Wings over the Rockies Museum in a 163,000-square-foot restored hangar on what was Lowry Air Force Base. It is filled with reminders of the military and aviation past of a base converted to a thriving residential, retail, and office neighborhood. The military's mighty contributions to Denver and Aurora's growth are also evident in two Lowry landmark districts, with military buildings recycled for civilian purposes.

"When I was cutting hair and hearing a good story, I would reach back and turn on a tape recorder," barber Paul Stewart recalled in an interview. "Folks dropped in with stories, artifacts, photos. I put up displays in the barber shop as conversation pieces. I got so much stuff that I ran out of room." By the 1970s, Stewart gave up barbering to devote more time to his museum. His collection outgrew the barbershop storefront, and he moved to various homes before settling in the Black American West Museum in the restored house of Dr. Justina Ford. Denver's pioneer black physician, Dr. Ford lived and practiced in this house. Unlike most doctors, she would make home visits and accept anything—or nothing—in payment from poor women of color she assisted in delivering some eight thousand babies. When her home faced demolition in 1983, preservationists moved it to 3901 California Street.

Jewish history is preserved in the Mizel Museum of Judaica. Opened in 1982 in the BMH Synagogue, it moved in 2004 to 400 South Kearney Street, where it offers permanent and temporary exhibits dealing with local, national, and international people and events. Some two dozen different Denver museums cover many topics, from the history of firefighters to that of cable television, which has its national center and museum in Denver. History and historical resources are preserved in several notable research libraries. The Denver Public Library's Western History and Genealogy Department has the strongest collection of books, manuscripts, photos, maps, and other materials on Denver and Colorado to be found anywhere. The Stephen Hart Library at History Colorado, the Colorado State Archives, the archives at the Auraria Library, and the archives at the University of Denver are also rewarding.

Denver's six suburban counties (Adams, Arapahoe, Boulder, Broomfield, Douglas, and Jefferson) have all also embraced history in order to give their citizens a sense of place and community.

Arvada

Arvada is a pacesetting suburb in showcasing its history, along with music concerts, plays, art, and special events, at the Arvada Center for the Arts and Humanities, the largest of the suburban museums and cultural centers. Along Ralston Creek, a tributary of Clear Creek, Arvada has established Gold Strike Park at the site where the Ralston party from Georgia made the first documented discovery of gold in the Denver area in 1850, eight years ahead of the Russell find that ignited the great Colorado gold rush. As a reminder of the town's grainy beginnings, the Arvada Historical Society has restored the Arvada Pride Flour Mill as a museum. The Arvada Historical Society also champions the Crescent Grange Hall and a Main Street revitalization program. Main Street (Wadsworth Boulevard) anchors a downtown National Register Historic District that encompasses typical small-town fixtures: a bank, a bakery, a stationery store, and taverns, with its signature water tower looming overhead.

Aurora

A sense of community has been fostered by the Aurora History Commission, created in 1970. That commission oversaw the opening of the Aurora History Museum in 1979 and the establishment of the Aurora Historic Preservation Commission, which has designated more than twenty-five local landmarks. The Gully Homestead, Coal Creek Schoolhouse, and DeLaney Round Barn have been restored as historical attractions in the DeLaney Farm Historic District and Park. On East Colfax, the old art-deco Fox Theatre has been converted to the Aurora Fox Arts Center.

On the Fitzsimons Army Hospital campus, now reborn as the University of Colorado's Anschutz Medical Campus, Aurora has landmarked the twin-entry guardhouses at the corner of East Colfax Avenue and Peoria Street in the Mission Revival style as the original celebratory entrance to the army medical complex, opened in 1918. The Red Cross Building, designed in the shape of a cross, was demolished, as Aurora's landmark ordinance, unlike Denver's, cannot prevent demolitions. The main hospital, a.k.a. Building 500, the largest building in Colorado when opened in 1941, is a National Register Landmark. This art-deco, ten-story beauty of limestone, aluminum, and glass features open-air decks for fresh air, heliotherapy, and fine views. Despite many newer, taller buildings erupting around it in recent years, it remains the most handsome building on campus and is the chosen home of the university administrators.

Boulder

Boulder, like Denver, has been a front-runner in preserving its landmarks and vintage neighborhoods. The Boulder Historic Preservation Program has designated more than 162 individual landmarks and ten historic districts, protecting more than thirteen hundred properties. One district, the Pearl Street Mall, has become the town's activity center. Another district, the Quadrangle at the heart of the University of Colorado campus, is considered the centerpiece of the nation's best example of consistent fine campus architecture, with fitting use of local sandstone and a distinctive red-tile roof, Tuscan style. Boulder's Chautauqua, founded in 1898, is a twenty-six-acre retreat containing ninety-eight cottages, rental lodges, a performing arts center, a community house, a year-round restaurant, and a history/archives museum as well as hiking trails. Of hundreds of Chautauquas once sprinkled across America, this is the second-best preserved after the New York State original.

Broomfield

A few souvenirs of Broomfield's corny past linger, including the Grange Hall at 7901 West 120th Avenue and two grain elevators along the railroad tracks. Broomfield's restored Colorado and Southern Railway Depot Museum is unusual in containing living quarters for the station agent and his family. The depot grounds contain a historic honey house, pump house, and a WPA sanitary outhouse. Although thousands of these new, improved outdoor toilets were made with their snap-shut doors, lack of windows, and movable construction, few survive, especially in restored condition. Researchers also trek to 17101 Huron Street in Broomfield to use the resources of the National Archives at Denver, which holds sixty thousand reels of microfilm and fifty thousand cubic feet of records created by federal agencies.

Commerce City

Rusty the Rabbit, most people thought, died on June 28, 2008, when the mechanical bunny ran his last race at Mile High Kennel Club in Commerce City. Starting in 1949, the mechanical wonder sped around the dog track, chased by greyhounds. Thousands watched each summer and sometimes bet nearly a million dollars in a single evening. When Mile High closed, Rusty was left to rust until he was rescued by volunteers from the Commerce City Historical Society. By late 2014 he had a new home at 6505 East Sixtieth Avenue, where the society also displayed memorabilia from Adams City High School and other artifacts.

With many of its collections in storage, Commerce City hopes someday to raise millions of dollars to buy a larger hutch for Rusty.

Englewood

The house of Englewood founder Thomas Skerritt narrowly escaped the wrecking ball to be restored for adaptive reuse. Another Englewood favorite, the Cherrelyn streetcar is enshrined in the Englewood town center in facsimile. The replica includes the single horse that pulled this rickety contraption uphill from Denver to Englewood and then rested on the rear platform of the coach for the ride back downhill into Denver. Old Dobbin, old-timers claim, was a smart horse who, unlike some bus drivers today, would stop automatically when he saw passengers waiting along the South Broadway car line.

Englewood offers one of Colorado's most unusual National Register Historic Districts in the Arapahoe Acres residential subdivision, an enclave between East Bates and East Dartmouth Avenues, bounded on the west by South Marion Street and on the east by South Franklin Street. Homes built there between 1949 and 1957 provide the metro area's best examples of consistent international and Usonian-style architecture. Its 124 modern homes of natural stone, brick, block, wood, and glass are unified by a palette of earth-tone colors and low-slung horizontal shapes. Architect Frank Lloyd Wright's work inspired the designers, including Eugene Sternberg, one of the most prolific and articulate of Colorado's modernists.

Golden

Above Golden, Lookout Mountain, one of the earliest and best-known segments of the Denver Mountain Park system, gained special significance when Denver laid to rest there the remains of William Frederick "Buffalo Bill" Cody (1846–1917). This western icon outperformed all the others; he taught the world to think of Americans as cowboys and Indians. Cast as a mythical hero in his lifetime, he became the star of stage plays, movies, 557 dime novels, and his own Wild West show, which entertained, among thousands of others, Queen Victoria and Kaiser Wilhelm II. Heroes of one generation often become the next generation's target practice. Buffalo Bill stayed in the saddle longer than most, although debunkers began gnawing on him in the 1920s. By the 1980s, he was being shot full of holes, and in recent years he has been written off by many scholars as a white male-chauvinist fraud, a violent bigot who slaughtered animals and Native Americans. Ironically, Indians he helped put on reservations found jobs with Cody, traveling the United States and Europe as performers with his Wild West show.

Frederick G. Bonfils and Harry H. Tammen, publishers of the *Denver Post,* reckoned Buffalo Bill a great tourist attraction. Tammen made Cody the star of the *Post*'s Sells-Floto Circus, although the creaky, bewigged hero had to be lifted onto his horse. In his declining years, Cody lived with his sister at 2932 Lafayette Street, now a designated Denver landmark. There on January 10, 1917, the Sir Galahad of the plains crossed over the Great Divide. Some twenty-five thousand people viewed his corpse as it lay in state at the Colorado state capitol, and five months later an equal number joined the funeral procession to the top of Lookout Mountain. Untold thousands of pilgrims have driven up the mountain to visit the grave of the poor farm boy who grew up to be America's most celebrated westerner.

As befits one of the state's oldest and most historic towns, Golden has rich historical and cultural resources. In addition to its reborn Main Street and Clear Creek History Park with a collection of old log buildings in the center of town, it hosts a half-dozen historical and cultural attractions, including the Foothills Arts Center, the Golden History Museum, the Astor House, the Colorado School of Mines Geological Museum, and the Rocky Mountain Quilt Museum. In recent decades, Golden has transformed once-neglected Clear Creek into trails and parks. Sculpturing the creek has facilitated kayaking and tubing as downtown amusements. Another major attraction is the biggest and best rail museum in the Rockies, the Colorado Railroad Museum, with a huge diorama, a garden railway, and restored standard- and narrow-gauge trains operating on excursions around the grounds.

Lakewood

The Lakewood Heritage Center at 801 South Yarrow Street has grown from a tiny museum in the old Belmar-estate calf barn to a complex of imported structures ranging from the 1869 Ralston schoolhouse to a

1930s-style ranch house, the Hallack-Webber residence. This unusual history park showcases six transplanted 1900s structures. Unlike many museums, which focus on the rich and famous and their homes, Lakewood has carved out a special niche—ordinary life and ordinary people of the twentieth century. The relocated and restored buildings include Gil and Ethel Gomez's joint Barbershop and Beauty Salon, the Valentine Diner, and a 1920s country school.

Gil and Ethel Gomez's Barbershop and Beauty Salon exemplifies the Lakewood Heritage Center's efforts to showcase the history of ordinary people. Photo by Tom Noel.

Littleton

Littleton's Historical Museum at 6028 South Gallup Street, one of the oldest and best financed in the metro area, ranks among the top local museums in the United States. Realizing that museums are for all the people, Littleton grants free admission to its displays, drawn from its collection of some forty thousand artifacts. Besides a collection of historic buildings, the thirty-nine-acre museum grounds include two living history farms, with chickens, cows, horses, mules, pigs, and sheep. Nearby, the house of Colorado's most exotic architect, Jules Jacques Benoit Benedict, is now a Carmelite convent. Littleton hired Benedict to design its exquisite beaux arts–style public library in 1916 and an even more fanciful Renaissance Revival–style town hall. The library has been reincarnated as a restaurant and the town hall as a theater. To deal with a decaying part of the old downtown, Littleton launched one of the first suburban urban-renewal programs. The blighted zone was leveled to become the campus of Arapahoe Community College, which opened in 1965.

Westminster

Westminster has revived part of its old main street, the 3900 block of West Seventy-Third Avenue, complete with a restored Red and White Grocery Store, the Rodeo Super Market, and the Westminster Grange Hall. This Grange Hall, like so many of that now endangered species, served as the community center for agricultural hamlets. The nearby Penguin Building, 7265 Lowell Boulevard, housed the pharmacy, soda fountain, and post office, with two landmarked schools across the street. Portions of the Church Ranch have been restored, including its well, which served pioneer travelers along the Cherokee Trail when Church's Stage Stop was the 1860s hub of what is now Westminster.

Westminster has twenty-one local, state, and national landmarks to celebrate, including the almost demolished Shoenberg Farm at 7231 Sheridan Boulevard, which supplied Denver's National Jewish Hospital. Shoenberg Farm evolved into one of the largest egg-dairy complexes in the US West and then became the Dolly Madison Ice Cream farm and headquarters. Westminster has one of Colorado's funkiest landmarks—the Savery Savory Mushroom Farm Water Tower at 11000 Federal Boulevard. Charles Savery came to Denver in 1909 to try mining but soon switched to mushrooms. He started out in Denver, but because of the enormous amount of manure required, many complaints led to Savery's banishment to Adams County. There his murky, stinky, unsavory kingdom thrived, growing into thirty-nine large buildings—the so-called caves. Savery opened branches in Los Angeles, San Francisco, and Missouri and by the mid-1930s produced ten thousand pounds of mushrooms a day. With Savery's death in 1960, his business also died. The restored and repainted tower is the sole remnant of a once vast agricultural empire in the suburb that has mushroomed into Colorado's ninth-largest city.

Public Art

Many communities have adopted public art programs in the past few decades. In 1988 Denver adopted an ordinance that set aside 1 percent of any city capital-improvement project over one million dollars for public art. Many more pieces date from Mayor Robert W. Speer's City Beautiful era, which focused on the classical idea of combining art with architecture, especially statues and murals, as exemplified in Denver's Civic Center. Private parties have also donated many works to Denver's Arts and Venues Department, which oversees more than three hundred works.

The most controversial creation, *Blue Mustang,* is a thirty-two-foot fiberglass blue stallion with glaring red eyes rearing on a hilltop at Denver International Airport. Also known as the Devil Horse, Blucifer, and Satan's Stallion, it fell on and killed its creator, New Mexico artist Luis Jiménez, in 2006. Prominently sited along Speer Boulevard on the Denver Performing Arts Complex lawn, Jonathan Borofsky's *Dancers* (2003) is a pair of skinny white fiberglass sixty-foot cavorting humanoids. The city's best-loved piece of public art is the Big Blue Bear, whose actual title is *I See What You Mean* (2003), a reference to its position peering into the Colorado Convention Center at Fourteenth and California Streets. Sculptor Lawrence Argent, chair of the University of Denver's Sculpture Department, created the forty-foot, lapis lazuli–blue bruin of cast polymer concrete and fiberglass triangles—four thousand of them—that make it look almost furry. "I toyed with what represents Colorado," Argent recalled. "Playing with my two kids and their teddy bears one day, it came to me."

Argent also produced two of the best-known suburban artworks. Recalling Aurora's days as a streetcar suburb, *Ghost Trolley* (2007) is an illuminated skinny, glassy trolley car on the median strip of East Colfax Avenue in old-town Aurora. His *Vivere* (2003) is a twenty-foot-tall clump of bright-green grass welcoming motorists on South Broadway to Englewood. Golden has adorned its Washington Avenue main street with sculptures of famous residents, such as Buffalo Bill Cody and Adolph Coors. Westminster boasts more than one hundred pieces of public art. Statues such as Louisville's *Coal Miner* and Thornton's *Fire*

Fighter celebrate local history. Many other communities are also venturing into public art as a way to promote civic identity and pride.

The area's museums and historic districts give it a glimpse into its past and a foundation upon which to build for the future. Its public art, like its past, provides it a sense of identity. Having grown so fast that it often did not honor its past, the city has come to recognize that a community uncertain of its heritage cannot function well. At least some citizens know that history is more than entertainment, fluff, and window dressing. Librarians, archivists, preservationists, authors—many of them volunteers—are often overlooked community heroes, for without them we would not have our past, and without our past we would not know where we have been, who we were, and who we are.

Chapter Fifteen

Paths to Tomorrow

*D*uring the 2010s, Denver was among the ten fastest-growing metro areas in the nation, with the seven-county region expected to reach 3.3 million people by 2020. The core city, unlike many other urban hubs, also mushroomed, with projections of topping 700,000 residents by 2020.

For more than 150 years, Denver's geography has allowed it to grow in all directions. Today the only serious barriers to expansion are the Front Range mountains, but, especially along the I-70 and US 285 corridors, they too are being peppered with people. Partly because of its central location and because transportation routes serve it well, the core city has remained alive, with many high-rises, offices, cultural attractions, and sports, dining, and entertainment venues concentrated downtown.

Although apartments and condominiums abound in central Denver and in portions of some suburban areas, most of the metropolis's

Denver's ups and downs are reflected in the skyline and also in this Elitch Gardens kiddie coaster. The skyline is still dominated by three fifty-story buildings erected during the late 1970s and early 1980s oil boom. Photo by Tom Noel.

residents, committed to the western ideal of elbow room, live in single-family detached houses with ample yards and plenty of grass to water and mow. In the past twenty years, some in-fill projects, such as Stapleton (on the site of the former Stapleton Airport), Lowry (on the site of Lowry Air Force Base), and Belmar (on the site of Villa Italia Shopping Center in Lakewood), have bucked the bucolic norm by promoting density and sacrificing yards to satisfy homeowners wanting ample interior square feet and developers wanting maximum profits. A desire for spacious homes in affluent neighborhoods both in the city and in the suburbs has led to modest houses on large lots being razed and replaced by large edifices. By 2015 such demolitions caused some long-term residents of Cherry Hills Village to fear they were losing their semirural ambience. At least if they decided to sell their homes, they could anticipate getting a good price in a village where owners often asked for more than five million dollars.

The drive for growth has been a constant. Sam Hoffman, the developer of Thornton in the early 1950s, was a twentieth-century version of William Larimer Jr., who founded Denver in 1858. Palmer Hoyt, editor of the *Denver Post* from 1946 to 1970, was a booster in the tradition of William Byers, founder of the *Rocky Mountain News* in 1859. And in every era, growth has come with challenges, including providing internal and external transportation, supplying water, and dealing with disasters and crime.

Transportation

As population and sprawl have grown, so has traffic. Denverites' love affair with cars first budded in 1898, when David Brunton, a mining engineer and inventor, assembled an automobile from a kit. Soon the city was paving more of its main streets and pondering ways to regulate motor vehicles. It even undertook to construct mountain touring roads, including the country's highest paved auto road, to the summit of 14,264-foot Mount Evans. Besides providing scenic trips for locals, the mountain highways attracted out-of-state tourists, which Denver welcomed between 1915 and 1930 by allowing them to camp in some city parks. In 1919 Colorado became one of the first four states to tax gasoline sales to help finance roads. By the 1990s, the initial tax of a cent a gallon had risen to twenty cents. From fewer than 6,000 cars registered in the city in 1910, the number skyrocketed to more than 375,015 in 1990. In 2014 drivers drove more than 24 million miles each day on the metro area's interstate highways.

The metro area's first modern four-lane, limited-access highway, West Sixth Avenue, was created in 1941–42 to whisk thousands of munitions workers from central Denver to the Denver Ordnance Plant at Sixth and Kipling. Another early freeway, the Denver-Boulder Turnpike (1952) was not free. Yet it proved so popular that tolls were removed in 1967 after the road paid for itself ahead of schedule. Although 11.2 miles of I-25, locally known as the Valley Highway, Colorado's north–south interstate highway, were completed through Denver in late 1958, it took another eleven years until I-25 ran all the way from Colorado's northern border to its southern. Finishing I-70, which opened its first Denver segment in 1964, took even longer. A milestone was reached in 1973 with completion of the 1.7-mile Eisenhower Tunnel, which allowed motorists to travel under the Continental Divide rather than over Loveland Pass. The road got even better in 1979 when the Johnson Tunnel, paralleling Eisenhower, was completed. I-70's march into western Colorado triggered an avalanche of development—strip malls, time-shares, ski areas— from Dillon to Glenwood Springs.

Between the 1940s and the early 1970s, developers and boosters touted highways as dynamos of progress. The yea-sayers faced little metro-area opposition, except from some displaced landowners and local residents, such as those in Globeville, Swansea, and Elyria, who resented having their neighborhoods sliced, diced, and polluted by I-70. In the 1970s, Denver's smog, much of it produced by cars, began to rival Los Angeles's. Despite the brown cloud that often smothered the region, highway proponents swatted naysayers like mosquitoes and built the freeways anyway, including I-225 (1964–76) in Aurora. By connecting I-25 with I-70, it gave some drivers a speedy way to bypass the congested I-25 stretch running through the central city, but eventually I-225 was clogged by congestion, created by the growth it generated.

Richard D. Lamm's election as Colorado's governor in 1972 temporarily gave effective voice to those who questioned constant road building and consequent urban sprawl. Fearing that a proposed I-470 linking

I-25 south of Denver with I-70 west of the city would lead to explosive growth in the southwestern outskirts of the metropolitan area and to increased air pollution that respected no boundaries, Lamm promised to drive a "silver stake" into the road and to shift its funds to mass transit. The stake did not stick. Like Dracula, the highway rose from the dead, as C-470 connected to toll road E-470 and other highways to make a nearly continuous beltway around Denver. As Lamm predicted, it fostered tremendous grown in the south metro region on what had been farm- and ranchland. Later antihighway salvos from environmentalists and Golden residents who loathed the thought of a highway barreling through their town stalled plans to complete a northern and western loop that, by interconnecting with E-470 and C-470, would create a continuous-ring highway. I-225, C-470, and E-470 all contributed substantially to the eastern metro-area boom that may give Aurora more population than Denver in ten or twenty years.

In 1991 the Colorado Department of Highways became the Colorado Department of Transportation (CDOT). The name change was inspired by the federal passage of the Intermodal Surface Transportation Efficiency Act, which mandated that states plan for all forms of surface transportation, including mass transit, rail, and bicycle. Yet freeway construction remained CDOT's top priority, which, as traffic grew increasingly congested, launched the Transportation Expansion Project (T-REX), a 2001–6 endeavor costing more than a billion and a half dollars, to remake and enlarge I-25 from downtown Denver to Douglas County. Instead of limiting highway construction or the number of cars, Colorado, forced to act by the federal government, tried to improve metro air quality by mandating auto-emissions inspections, which began in 1981.

CDOT did work closely with the Regional Transportation District (RTD) to include a light-rail line into the T-REX design. Denver's first modern light-rail line, a 5.3-mile stretch from downtown to South Denver, opened in 1994. In ensuing years, metro voters, with some exceptions, have dedicated part of the sales taxes they pay to subsidizing construction of FasTracks rail lines. This path to the future mirrors the solution of a hundred years ago when the city enjoyed an extensive street railway network and interurban connections to towns outside of

Denver, such as Broomfield, Boulder, Lafayette, and Superior. By the mid-twentieth century, the rail system had been abandoned—the Denver Tramway ran its last streetcar on June 3, 1950. By 2016 RTD's rail lines, most of which converged at Union Station in downtown Denver, encompassed more than 75 miles, reaching as far southeast as Lincoln Avenue in Douglas County, as far south as West Mineral Avenue in Littleton, as far west as the fringes of Golden, as far northwest as Wheat Ridge, as far north as Westminster, and as far east as Denver International Airport. By 2016 transit advocates could point to increases in population density near RTD stations, a glimmer of hope in the seemingly futile war against sprawl.

At considerably less expense than RTD, which spent billions on its projects, bicyclists also did their part to cut down on auto traffic. Like light rail, cycling has deep local roots—the first known Denver cyclist rode a velocipede on Blake Street in 1869. With the advent of "safety" bicycles, essentially the same as today's models, men and women pursued cycling with a passion. By 1900, according to historian James Whiteside in his book *Colorado: A Sports History,* Denver's forty thousand bicycles allowed it to brag that it had more cycles per capita than any other city in the country. Throttled by automobiles and mid-twentieth-century traffic engineers, who seemingly regarded cyclists as nuisances, bicycling declined until enthusiasts revived it by lobbying for dedicated bicycle lanes, particularly in Boulder and Denver. To put even more bikes in those lanes, the city in 2009 launched one of the nation's first large-scale, city-wide bike-sharing programs, Denver B-cycle.

Aerotropolis

Billions of dollars for highways and rapid transit kept the metro area's internal transportation system functioning, if not perfectly, at least as well as in many other large US cities. In the twenty-first century, as in the area's earlier history, external transportation was also a critical component of the region's prosperity. Faced with vast distances to other national urban centers, Denverites have for more than a half century relied heavily on air travel. The city's struggle to become the region's major rail hub in the nineteenth century and its twentieth-century work to become a major air hub have been key elements in making it the most important metropolis in the Rocky Mountain region and one of the nation's major cities.

Thousands watched as French aviator Louis "Birdman" Paulhan, the first person to fly an airplane in Denver, took short flights at Overland Park in early February 1910. Eight months later, on November 17, spectators at Overland saw twenty-four-year-old daredevil Ralph Johnstone plunge to his death, giving him the sad distinction of being the first professional pilot killed in an airplane crash in the United States. Nearly two decades passed before Denver Municipal Airport opened in 1929 on the northeast outskirts, near Thirty-Second Avenue (now Martin Luther King Jr. Boulevard) and Quebec Street. It was renamed Stapleton Airport in 1944, to honor Mayor Benjamin Stapleton, an early advocate of the field. Renamed Stapleton International Airport in 1964, it actually became international four years later with the launch of nonstop flights to Calgary, Canada. By the 1980s, it had become one of the ten busiest US airports. Boosters, led by Denver mayor Federico Peña, seized upon complaints about noise, inadequate runways, and congestion at Stapleton to push for construction of a new facility. To no avail, critics bemoaned billions of dollars in construction and financing costs and advocated cheaper alternatives. Denver International Airport (DIA), after embarrassing delays to get a functioning baggage-handling system, finally opened in 1995.

With its 53-square-mile site, DIA is the nation's largest airport in terms of area. Its Jeppesen Terminal boasts a distinctive Teflon-coated fiberglass tent top with soaring white cones, resembling the snowcapped Rockies as well as Native American tepees. A 2015 airport hotel on the south side of the terminal awkwardly blocked the entry view of the iconic tents. The DIA added a sixth runway in 2003 that is sixteen thousand feet long and able to accommodate the latest jumbo jets. The DIA has become the nation's sixth-busiest airport and the world's thirteenth busiest. Recently, Michael B. Hancock, who succeeded John W. Hickenlooper Jr. as Denver's mayor in 2011, has dreamed of an aerotropolis at the airport, a megacomplex embracing hotels, business parks, a golf course, a conference center, greenhouses, auction grounds for heavy equipment, and even a wildlife viewing area. In November 2015, the dream took a step toward reality when voters in Denver and Adams Counties approved measures to fund airport development and share tax revenues.

Two other significant airports serve the metro area. Arapahoe County Airport has sprawled into adjacent Douglas County and been renamed Centennial Airport. It has become the third-busiest general aviation airport in the United States and the thirtieth busiest among all US airports in terms of total operations (landings and takeoffs). Jefferson County Airport also grew when other surrounding counties fed it business and was renamed Rocky Mountain Metropolitan Airport.

Seeking Water

Creating cities in Front Range drylands was not only a matter of providing good transportation. Without annually bringing in billions of gallons of water, the metropolis could not sustain millions of people. Up to the mid-1930s, the city depended heavily upon the South Platte. Knowing the river would eventually not sustain growth, the Denver Water Board, which took over the privately owned Denver Union Water Company in 1918, lusted after water from Colorado west of the Continental Divide, where most of state's water is found, largely because of snowfall in the mountains. In the 1930s, the DWB persuaded the federal Public Works Administration to help finance diversion of western slope water through the 6.1-mile Pioneer Bore, a tunnel that parallels the Moffat Tunnel, 45 miles northwest of the city. By 1936 water from the Fraser River, which previously flowed into the Colorado River, was tumbling toward the Mile High City.

The Moffat diversion, the first large-scale transfer of western slope water to the eastern slope, relieved Denver's water worries until the 1960s, when population growth and drought again prompted the DWB to lap up more western slope water by building Dillon Reservoir, 68 miles west of the city. It stored Blue River water that gushed through the 23.3-mile Harold Roberts Tunnel to the North Fork of the South Platte. In another massive diversion, the US Bureau of Reclamation financed the Colorado–Big Thompson Project, which moves water from the upper reaches of the Colorado River through the 13.1-mile Alva B. Adams Tunnel (1947) to water northeastern Colorado farms and hundreds of thousands of people in Boulder, Louisville, and other northern portions of the metropolitan area. When western slope residents complained about water moving east, wags on the eastern slope joked that Coors was improving water at its Golden brewery and returning it to western Colorado in shiny gold and silver cans of much-improved H$_2$O.

Moffat Tunnel and Dillon water gave the DWB power over many of Denver's suburbs. Sometimes it agreed to supply water; sometimes, especially in drought periods, it turned off the spigot. It charged suburban users more than it did Denver consumers, justifying the difference because Denver rate payers had provided much of the money to purchase, expand, and maintain the expensive system. Although the DWB was an entity separate from the City and County of Denver, many suburbs and developers saw it as a Denver cat's-paw.

Dillon gave the DWB sufficient water to allow considerable suburban growth, but some suburbs did not want to bet their futures on the willingness or the ability of the Denver Water Board to supply them. Englewood was among the first to declare its independence by building McLellan Reservoir, near Santa Fe Drive (US 85) and West County Line Road in the early 1950s. Aurora spent hundreds of millions of dollars to give its citizens and developers an expanding and dependable water supply. In partnership with Colorado Springs, it built the Homestake Project, which began diverting western slope water in 1967. Homestake, along with numerous other Aurora projects, including the Rampart Range Pipeline (1981), Aurora Reservoir (1989), and the $653-million Prairie Waters Project (2010), captures, moves, purifies, and reuses water.

To allow for decades of additional development, particularly in the suburbs, the Denver Water Board and its suburban counterparts cooperated in the 1980s to plan a 1.1-million-acre-foot reservoir—four times the capacity of Dillon—on the South Platte, near Deckers. Environmental groups and thirsty out-of-state water users fought the proposal, and in 1990 the US Environmental Protection Agency killed it. Partly by conserving water and partly by developing other sources, the metropolis sailed through the 1990s without Two Forks. But suffering a severe drought in 2002 with only 7.48 inches of precipitation (less than half the yearly norm) and in 2006 with less than 9.00 inches of moisture, some planners rued Two Forks's demise and hoped to revive it on a smaller scale. Planners also considered storing perhaps as much as 150 million acre-feet of water underground in Denver Basin aquifers. Residents of Douglas County subdivisions, many of whom depended upon wells, likely found underground storage ideas appealing because by the early twenty-first century, they were forced to dig deeper and deeper for the precious fluid.

Lakes and Waterways

The region's quest for water and its efforts to control floods led to the creation of reservoirs and waterways that not only slaked people's thirst and grew their grass but also gave them fishing, boating, swimming, and other recreational opportunities. Aurora Reservoir and many others, such as Antero, Carter Lake, Dillon, Gross, Lake Granby, Spinney Mountain, and Tarryall, spread over a vast region, owe their existence to carefully planned storage projects. Cherry Creek Reservoir, on the other hand, came to be when water backed up behind Cherry Creek Dam, which was built in 1950 to stop Cherry Creek from periodically washing away parts of the city, as it did in 1864, 1875, 1878, and 1912. On August 3, 1933, the usually meek creek became a torrent when the Castlewood Dam east of Castle Rock collapsed, releasing a large lake into the little stream. The South Platte River also occasionally flooded, but most people ignored the threat until June 16, 1965, when, swollen by a 14-inch downpour that inundated Sedalia and other places south of the city, the river rushed north, killing at least twenty-six people, drowning race horses at Centennial Race Track in Littleton, washing out many major bridges, and doing a half-billion dollars in damage.

The 1965 disaster prompted the building of Chatfield Dam and Reservoir, southwest of Denver. It also spurred leaders, including Denver mayor William H. McNichols Jr., Joe Shoemaker, and others, to clean up the trashy banks of the South Platte. Shoemaker, who had been Denver manager of public works and then a state senator, described the unpalatable Platte in his book *Returning the Platte to the People:*

> Instead of a place to stroll or listen to a band on a summer
> evening, the Platte became . . . a place for slaughter houses
> and railyards, storm water discharges and trash discards. . . .
> Off to the river we went with salt-laden snow from the

downtown pavements. . . . When old pavement was broken up to be replaced, the great jagged chunks were used to line the river to prevent erosion of its banks. . . . [W]e also turned to the automobile junkyard for ballast and decorated the river with wrecks. . . . When diesel locomotives needed oil changes they were driven to a yard besides man's favorite dump, the South Platte, and the dirty lubrication was released like a flood into the ground. When the soil and substratum were fully saturated, the horrid gunk oozed sideways, out of the banks and into the river.

Using public and private money, Shoemaker and the Platte River Development Committee, founded in 1974, spruced up portions of the river and created Confluence Park at the junction of the South Platte and Cherry Creek. It opened on July 4, 1976, as the first of many greenswards that now line the river and its tributaries and even penetrate into the mountains in Waterton Canyon, where hikers and bicyclists follow the old path of the Denver, South Park & Pacific Railroad. North of Denver, Adams County has groomed a greenway along the South Platte, where abandoned quarries and sand-dredging pits are now lakes and ponds. From the river, side trails follow tributaries, such as Sand Creek and Clear Creek. In Jefferson County, paths parallel Clear and Ralston Creeks, which teased early-day prospectors with their golden sands. Golden has transformed its once unclear Clear Creek into history and water parks, where tourists can pan for gold, tour a log village, or kayak the white water. The Highline Canal, flowing through Littleton, Denver, Centennial, and Aurora, has similarly been made into a tree-lined trail, despite occasional Denver Water Board complaints that it annually wastes millions of gallons through seepage and evaporation.

Optimists think that Chatfield and Cherry Creek will prevent major floods, and developers keep inching closer and closer to the rivers. Pessimists recall the 1935 floods in eastern Colorado, which turned the Republican River into a monster as wide as the Mississippi in parts of Nebraska. They warn that two dams and miles of greenways may not protect the metropolis. Those warnings hit home in September 2013 when Boulder, drenched with seventeen inches of rain in seven days, suffered devastating floods, as did other nearby towns, such as Lyons and Longmont.

Tourism

Waterway beautification enhanced Denver's second-largest industry: tourism. The Colorado Tourism Office and VISIT DENVER: The Visitors and Convention Bureau spend millions each year luring tourists. Denver has established itself as a destination city, capturing more than 13 million tourists annually who spend an estimated four billion dollars. Tourism spiked in 1993 when some 186,000 people from all over the globe converged on the Mile High City for a visit by Pope John Paul II for World Youth Day. A record crowd descended on Cherry Creek State Park for his final Mass. The international spotlight shone on the city again in June 1997 when it hosted the Summit of the Eight, which brought Bill Clinton, Britain's Tony Blair, and Russia's Boris Yeltsin and other world leaders to the Queen City. Yet more hoopla, visitation, and international publicity came in 2008 with the Democratic National Convention that nominated Barack Obama for his successful run for the presidency.

Beer Town

Brewers claim that many visitors are drawn by the bubbling beer industry. Since 2006, when it rolled out 23,370,848 barrels, Colorado has produced more beer than any other state. Coors Brewing Company in Golden leads the pack. Following mergers with Molson of Montreal and Miller of Milwaukee, Coors remains the single-largest Colorado contender and claims that its Golden plant is the largest single-brewery plant in the world. But the giant is not alone. Today proliferating brewpubs and craft breweries soak the metro area.

Colorado craft brewing began in 1979 with the opening of the Boulder Brewing Company. Brewpubs had to wait for the Colorado General Assembly to allow breweries to sell this product on the premises. Taking advantage of that change in 1988, brewpub pioneer John W. Hickenlooper Jr., an out-of-work oil geologist, with three partners opened the Wynkoop Brewing Company in Lower Downtown Denver. It became an instant success and inspired many others to hop into the trade. Avery Brewing Company, founded in Boulder in 1993, became the first Colorado brewer to bottle an India pale ale. Oskar Blues Brewing Company in the small Boulder County town of Lyons broke new ground by marketing craft beer in cans, while the Left Hand Brewing Company in Longmont launched its Ales 4 FemAles.

Denver celebrates its frothy eminence with the Great American Beer Festival. From humble 1981 origins in Boulder, the GABF moved to Denver in 1984, where it has become America's largest such brew-haha, featuring 750 breweries by 2015. The metro area by 2015 boasted more than 50 brewpubs (with restaurants) and 100 craft breweries (with no food service except for food trucks). So no matter what the problems of traffic, water, air, congestion, and other urban difficulties, Denverites had a thousand different hometown beers to try out. Yet many chose to relax and get high in another way.

Pot Time in the Old Town

Giving new meaning to the old slogan "the Highest State," Coloradans voted to legalize medical marijuana in 2000 and added recreational pot in 2012. Denver has subsequently become a national leader in dealing with a burning issue. Be it teenagers on a lark or a family desperately in need of medical marijuana denied in their home state to soothe a dying, seizure-ridden child, marijuana has, like ski slopes and sunshine, attracted newcomers.

Voters legalized recreational marijuana in 2012. Since then, pot has become one of Denver's fastest-growing industries and a tourist lure. Photo by Steve Leonard.

Pot has become big business. Practically every vacant warehouse has been snatched up for the four hundred or so grow operations feeding around two hundred metro-area retail outlets. As supplies grew like Jack's beanstalk, the average price of recreational cannabis dropped from sixty dollars per eighth ounce in 2014 to thirty-eight dollars in 2015. Anti-tax pot proponents claim this is still higher than the illegal black-market street price of untaxed cannabis and thus encourages criminal activity. Taxes on legal grass bring in around a hundred million dollars a year. Some of that money funds ads warning users that they cannot smoke it in parks, on the street, or in other public places; take dope out of state; or provide it to minors. In Colorado anyone over twenty-one years of age can possess up to an ounce of cannabis. Non-Colorado residents can purchase, and there is no registration system. Driving under the influence is illegal.

The Press, Crime, and the Future

Newspapers have long provided the first draft of the city's history. The oldest newspaper and a rich source, the *Rocky Mountain News* published its last edition on February 27, 2009, less than two months short of its 150th birthday. The *Denver Post* had won a long and bitter newspaper war. Yet even then the *Post* was eliminating many of its reporters and editors, as Internet sites siphoned advertising revenue away from the newspapers. Media gurus wonder if the anemic *Post* of today is still capable of adequately performing the civic watch-dog and community-building functions that it and the *Rocky Mountain News* provided for more than a century.

Both papers, for example, offered superb coverage of the April 20, 1999, massacre of twelve students and one teacher by two students, who then killed themselves, at Columbine High School in Jefferson County. In 2000 Tom Mauser, father of one of the Columbine victims, successfully campaigned to get Colorado voters to approve an amendment to the state constitution, mandating background checks of some gun purchasers. In 2003 progun legislators made carrying concealed weapons easier in the state. After a deranged shooter killed twelve people and wounded nearly sixty others on July 20, 2012, at an Aurora movie theater, gun-control advocates again called for reforms and persuaded the

Colorado General Assembly in 2013 to eliminate background-check loopholes and to forbid purchases of large-capacity ammunition magazines such as the one-hundred-round clip the Aurora killer had. Still, few, if any, deluded themselves into believing that Coloradans would never suffer another mass killing.

The metropolis, however, refused to be defined by its tragedies. Boosters boasted of core city preservation, construction projects, and recreational and economic opportunities. Voters in 2015 demonstrated their optimism by approving a massive redevelopment plan for the National Western Stock Show and its surrounding neighborhoods.

Born in the optimism of the 1859 gold rush, the city forged ahead in the early twenty-first century with the energy reminiscent of its past. Sprawl, traffic gridlock, pollution, water woes, drug addiction, scarcity of affordable housing, beggars on street corners, homeless men and women huddled on sidewalks near overflowing shelters, the soaring cost of higher education, and the decline of major newspapers worry some. Many others, however, envision a bright future of fishing, hiking, biking, skiing, playing soccer and volleyball, watching the Denver Broncos or Colorado Rockies, drinking a beer, mowing and watering their grass, or smoking it.

Selected Bibliography

This bibliography includes books that we have relied on or cited by title in the text as well as many works written since 1990. For hundreds of earlier books and articles, see the bibliography in Stephen J. Leonard and Thomas J. Noel, *Denver: Mining Camp to Metropolis.* Boulder: University Press of Colorado, 1990.

Abbott, Carl, Stephen J. Leonard, and Thomas J. Noel. *Colorado: A History of the Centennial State.* 5th (heavily revised) ed. Niwot: University Press of Colorado, 2013.

Abbott, Frank C. *The Auraria Higher Education Center: How It Came to Be.* Denver: Auraria Higher Education Center, 1999.

Abrams, Jeanne. *Dr. Charles David Spivak: A Jewish Immigrant and the American Tuberculosis Movement.* Boulder: University Press of Colorado, 2009.

Ackland, Len. *Making a Real Killing: Rocky Flats and the Nuclear West.* Albuquerque: University of New Mexico Press, 1999.

Amole, Gene. *Morning.* Denver: Denver Publishing, 1983.

Appleby, Susan C. *Fading Past: The Story of Douglas County, Colorado.* Palmer Lake, CO: Filter Press, 2001.

Arps, Louisa Ward. *Denver in Slices.* Denver: Sage Books, 1959. Reprint, Athens: Ohio University Press, 1998.

Bakemeier, Alice. *Country Club Heritage: A History and a Guide to a Denver Neighborhood.* Denver: Cranmer Park / Hilltop Civic Association, 1997.

Bean, Geraldine. *Charles Boettcher: A Study in Pioneer Western Enterprise.* Boulder: Westview Press, 1976.

Beaton, Gail M. *Colorado Women: A History.* Boulder: University Press of Colorado, 2012.

Bluemel, Elinor. *The Golden Opportunity: The Story of the Unique Emily Griffith Opportunity School of Denver.* Boulder: Johnson, 1965.

Bowen, Robert E. *The Vision, the Struggle: How Metropolitan State University Began*. Centennial, CO: REBALS Press, 2015.

Brettell, Richard B. *Historic Denver: The Architects and the Architecture, 1858–1893*. Denver: Historic Denver, 1973.

Brosnan, Kathleen A. *Uniting Mountain and Plain: Cities, Law, and Environmental Change Along the Front Range*. Albuquerque: University of New Mexico Press, 2002.

Brundage, David T. *The Making of Western Labor Radicalism: Denver's Organized Workers, 1878–1905*. Urbana: University of Illinois Press, 1994.

Bunyak, Dawn, Thomas H. Simmons, and R. Laurie Simmons. *Denver Area Post–World War II Suburbs*. Denver: Colorado Department of Transportation, 2011.

Chandler, Mary Voelz. *Guide to Denver Architecture with Regional Highlights*. 2nd ed. Golden, CO: Fulcrum, 2013.

Colorado Historical Society. *Colorado History* 5 (2001). This work includes articles relating to Denver: Jeanne Abrams, "Children Without Homes: The Plight of Denver's Orphans, 1880–1930"; Moya Hansen, "Pebbles on the Shore: Economic Opportunity in Denver's Five Points Neighborhood, 1920–1950"; and Franklin J. James and Christopher B. Gerboth, "A Camp Divided: Annexation Battles, the Poundstone Amendment, and Their Impact on Metropolitan Denver, 1941–1988."

Convery, William Joseph, III. *Pride of the Rockies: The Life of Colorado's Premier Irish Patron, John Kernan Mullen*. Boulder: University Press of Colorado, 2000.

de Baca, Vincent C., ed. *La Gente: Hispano History and Life in Colorado*. Niwot: University Press of Colorado and the Colorado Historical Society, 1999.

Denton, James A. *Rocky Mountain Radical: Myron W. Reed, Christian Socialist*. Albuquerque: University of New Mexico Press, 1997.

Dorsett, Lyle W., and G. Michael McCarthy. *The Queen City: A History of Denver*. Boulder: Pruett, 1986.

Downing, Sibyl, and Robert E. Smith. *Tom Patterson: Colorado Crusader for Change*. Niwot: University Press of Colorado, 1995.

Everett, Derek R. *The Colorado State Capitol: History, Politics, Preservation*. Boulder: University Press of Colorado, 2005.

Faulkner, Debra Benson. *Touching Tomorrow: The Emily Griffith Story*. Palmer Lake, CO: Filter Press, 2005.

Field, Kimberly, and Kelly Kordes Anton. *Westminster: The First 100 Years*. Westminster, CO: Westminster Centennial Committee, 2010.

Foster, Mark S. *Citizen Quigg: A Mayor's Life of Civic Service*. Golden, CO: Fulcrum, 2006.

Fowler, Gene. *Timber Line: A Story of Bonfils and Tammen*. New York: Covici, Friede, 1933.

French, Emily. *Emily: The Diary of a Hard Worked Woman*. Edited by Janet Lecompte. Lincoln: University of Nebraska Press, 1987.

Goldberg, Robert Alan. *Hooded Empire: The Ku Klux Klan in Colorado*. Urbana: University of Illinois Press, 1981.

Goodstein, Phil. Multiple volumes on many aspects of Denver history. Denver: New Social Publications, 1988–present.

Gould, Richard. *The Life and Times of Richard Castro: Bridging a Cultural Divide*. Denver: Colorado Historical Society, 2007.

Hafen, LeRoy Reuben. *Colorado and Its People: A Narrative and Topical History of the Centennial State*. New York: Lewis Historical, 1948.

Hendricks, Rickey, and Mark S. Foster. *For a Child's Sake: History of the Children's Hospital, Denver, Colorado, 1910–1990*. Niwot: University Press of Colorado, 1994.

History Colorado. "Denver Inside and Out." *Colorado History* (Colorado Historical Society) 16 (2011). This work includes short articles on early Denver railroads by Eric L. Clements; on the pioneer medical community by Rebecca Hunt; on early schools by Shawn Snow; on women in politics in the period 1893–97 by Marcia Tremmel Goldstein; on disorderly women by Cheryl Siebert Waite; on Colorado women in the Ku Klux Klan by Betty Jo Brenner; on Denver's early Jewish community by Jeanne Abrams; on the Bureau of Indians Affairs' Relocation Program and Denver's Native Americans by Azusa Ono; on Denver's recreational empire by Michael Childers; on summer homes by Melanie Shellenbarger; and on Cherry Creek by B. Erin Cole.

Hosokawa, William. *Thunder in the Rockies: The Incredible Denver Post*. New York: William Morrow, 1976.

Iversen, Kristen. *Full Body Burden: Growing Up in the Nuclear Shadow of Rocky Flats*. New York: Crown, 2012.

———. *Molly Brown: Unraveling the Myth*. Boulder: Johnson Books, 1999.

Kelly, George V. *The Old Gray Mayors of Denver*. Boulder: Pruett, 1974.

Kelsey, Harry E., Jr. *Frontier Capitalist: The Life of John Evans*. Denver: State Historical Society of Colorado / Pruett, 1969.

King, William M. *Going to Meet a Man: Denver's Last Legal Public Execution, 27 July 1886*. Niwot: University Press of Colorado, 1990.

Kreck, Dick. *Denver in Flames: Forging a New Mile High City.* Golden, CO: Fulcrum, 2000.

———. *Smaldone: The Untold Story of an American Crime Family.* Golden, CO: Fulcrum, 2009.

Leonard, Stephen J. *Trials and Triumphs: A Colorado Portrait of the Great Depression, with FSA Photographs.* Niwot: University Press of Colorado, 1993.

Limerick, Patricia Nelson, with Jason L. Hanson. *A Ditch in Time: The City, the West, and Water.* Golden, CO: Fulcrum, 2012.

Lindsey, Benjamin Barr, and Harvey J. O'Higgins. *The Beast.* New York: Doubleday, Page, 1910. Reprint, Boulder: University Press of Colorado, 2009.

MacMechen, Edgar C. *Robert W. Speer: A City Builder.* Denver: Smith-Brooks, 1919.

Mehls, Steven F., Carol J. Drake, and James E. Fell Jr. *Aurora: Gateway to the Rockies.* Aurora, CO: Cordillera Press, 1985.

Morley, Judy Mattivi. *Centennial Arvada, 1904–2004: A Pictorial History.* Virginia Beach: Donning, 2004.

Nelson, Sarah M., with K. Lynn Berry, Richard F. Carrillo, Bonnie J. Clark, Lorie E. Rhodes, and Dean Saitta. *Denver: An Archaeological History.* Boulder: University Press of Colorado, 2008.

Noel, Thomas J. *Colorado: A Historical Atlas.* Norman: University of Oklahoma Press, 2015.

———. *University of Colorado Hospital: A History.* Denver: University of Colorado Hospital Foundation, 2013.

Noel, Thomas J., and Dan W. Corson. *Boulder County: An Illustrated History.* Boulder: Historic Boulder, 1999.

Noel, Thomas J., and Debra B. Faulkner. *Mile High Tourism: Denver's Convention and Visitor History.* Denver: VISIT DENVER, the Convention and Visitor Bureau, and the Center for Colorado and the West, 2010.

Noel, Thomas J., and Nicholas J. Wharton. *Denver Landmarks and Historic Districts.* Boulder: University Press of Colorado, 2016.

Noel, Thomas J., and Amy Zimmer. *Showtime: Denver's Performing Arts, Convention Centers and Theatre District.* Denver: Denver Theatres and Arenas, 2008.

Norgren, Barbara J., and Thomas J. Noel. *Denver: The City Beautiful and Its Architects.* 1987. Reprint, Denver: Historic Denver, 1993.

Perkin, Robert L. *The First Hundred Years: An Informal History of Denver and the "Rocky Mountain News," 1859–1959.* New York: Doubleday, 1959.

Pettem, Silvia. *Broomfield: Changes Through Time.* Longmont, CO: Book Lode, 2001.

Philpott, William. *Vacationland: Tourism and Environment in the Colorado High Country*. Seattle: University of Washington Press, 2013.

Rex-Atzet, Wendy, Sally L. White, and Erika D. Walker, with photography by John Fielder. *Denver Mountain Parks: 100 Years of the Magnificent Dream*. Silverthorne, CO: Denver Mountain Parks / John Fielder, 2014.

Secrest, Luther Clark. *Hell's Belles: Denver's Brides of the Multitudes with Attention to Various Gamblers, Scoundrels, and Mountebanks and a Biography of Sam Howe, Frontier Lawman*. Aurora, CO: Hindsight Historical Publications, 1996.

Shellenbarger, Melanie. *High Country Summers: The Early Second Homes of Colorado, 1880–1940*. Tucson: University of Arizona Press, 2012.

Shoemaker, Joe, with Leonard A. Stevens. *Returning the Platte to the People*. Denver: Greenway Foundation, 1981.

Simmons, Thomas H., and R. Laurie. *Historic Residential Subdivisions of Metropolitan Denver, 1940–1965: National Register of Historic Places Multiple Property Documentation Form*. Denver: Colorado Historical Society, 2011.

Smiley, Jerome C. *History of Denver, with Outlines of the Earlier History of the Rocky Mountain Country*. Denver: Denver Times, Times-Sun, 1901.

Smith, Duane Allan. *Horace Tabor: His Life and the Legend*. 1973. Boulder: Colorado Associated University Press. Reprint, Boulder: University Press of Colorado, 1990.

Sternberg, Barbara, Jennifer Boone, and Evelyn Waldron. *Anne Evans, a Pioneer in Colorado's Cultural History: The Things That Last When Gold Is Gone*. Denver: Buffalo Park Press for the Center for Colorado and the West at Auraria Library, 2011.

Teeuwen, Randall C. *Growing Up Gates: A Family History*. Greenwood Village, CO: Bear Creek, 2002.

Tyler, Daniel. *The Last Waterhole in the West: The Colorado–Big Thompson Project and the Northern Colorado Water Conservancy District*. Niwot: University Press of Colorado, 1993.

Ubbelohde, Carl, Maxine Benson, and Duane A. Smith. *A Colorado History*. Boulder: Pruett, 2006.

West, Elliott. *The Contested Plains: Indians, Goldseekers and the Rush to Colorado*. Lawrence: University Press of Kansas, 1998.

Whiteside, James. *Colorado: A Sports History*. Niwot: University Press of Colorado, 1999.

About the Authors

A third-generation Denverite, STEPHEN J. LEONARD received a BA in history from Regis College–Denver, a MA from the University of Wyoming and a PhD from Claremont Graduate School. He is a Professor of History at Metropolitan State University of Denver, where he has taught since 1966. He has authored or coauthored half a dozen books and an equal number of articles on Colorado and/or Denver topics. He has served on various community groups, including the Denver Landmark Preservation Commission and the Board of Directors of Colorado Humanities.

THOMAS JACOB NOEL received a BA in history and an MA in library science from the University of Denver, and an MA and PhD in history from the University of Colorado at Boulder. He is a Professor of History and Director of Public History and Preservation at the University of Colorado at Denver and Director of the Center for Colorado Studies at the Denver Public Library. Tom is a columnist for the *Denver Post* and "Dr. Colorado" for KUSA Channel 9's *Colorado & Company*. Tom conducts walking tours of Denver neighborhoods, specializing in cemeteries, churches, libraries, saloons, and other prominent sites. He is the author or coauthor of forty-eight books, many dealing with Denver. He served on the Denver Landmark Preservation Commission and as its chair. For his books, classes, tours, and other information, check out dr-colorado.com.

Index

Westminster University, 131, 132

wheat processing, *see* flour milling

Wheat Ridge, 132–33

White Antelope, Chief, 9

White, Alma, 132

White, Edward, 114

White, Stanford, 131

Whitnah, Joseph, 58

Windsor Hotel, 61, 164

Wings Over the Rockies Museum, 169

Winkler, Eugene A. von, 43

Winter Park Ski Area, 76, 99, 158, 159

Wolfe Hall, 31

Women's Christian Temperance Union, 65

women's suffrage, xv, 64–65

Wootton, Richens "Uncle Dick," 19

Working Boys' Home and School, 36

Works Progress Administration, 94, 96, 97

World Series, 153

World War I, 81–84, 101

World War II, 101–4

World Youth Day, xvii, 152, 189

Wright, Frank Lloyd, 173

Wynkoop, Edward W., 8

Wynkoop Brewing Company, 189

yellow journalism, 68

Yeltsin, Boris, 189

Young, Eric, 153

Young Women's Christian Association, 36

Zaharias, George, 161

Zaharias, Mildred "Babe" Didrickson, 161

Zang, Adolph, 118